THE DOCTRINE OF
THE CHURCH

THE
DOCTRINE OF THE CHURCH

BY

A. C. A. HALL, D.D., LL.D.
BISHOP OF VERMONT

WIPF & STOCK · Eugene, Oregon

Wipf and Stock Publishers
199 W 8th Ave, Suite 3
Eugene, OR 97401

The Doctrine of the Church
By Hall, A. C. A.
ISBN 13: 978-1-5326-7102-9
Publication date 9/25/2018
Previously published by The University Press
at the University of the South, 1909

EDITOR'S PREFACE

THE object of this series is to provide for the clergy and laity of the Church a statement, in convenient form, of its Doctrine, Discipline and Worship — as well as to meet the often expressed desire on the part of Examining Chaplains for text-books which they could recommend to Candidates for Holy Orders.

To satisfy, on the one hand, the demand of general readers among the clergy and laity, the books have been provided with numerous references to larger works, making them introductory in their nature; and on the other hand, to make them valuable for use in canonical examinations, they have been arranged according to the Canons of the Church which deal with that matter.

It is the earnest hope of the collaborators in this series that the impartial scholarship and unbiased attitude adopted throughout, will commend themselves to Churchmen of all types, and that the books will therefore be accorded a general reception and adopted as far as possible as a *norm* for canonical examinations. The need of such a norm is well known to all.

And finally a word to Examining Chaplains. They will find that the volumes are so arranged that it will be possible to adapt them to all kinds of students. The actual text itself should be taken as the *minimum* of requirement from the Candidate, and then, by reference on their part to the bibliographies at the end of each chapter, they can increase as they see fit the amount of learning to be demanded in each case. It has been the endeavor of the editor to make these bibliographies so comprehensive that Examining Chaplains will always find suitable parallel readings.

If in any way the general public will be by this series encouraged to study the position of the Church, and if the canonical examinations in the different dioceses can be brought into greater harmony one with another, our object will be accomplished.

ARTHUR R. GRAY.

Easter, 1909.

PREFACE

A FEW words may be allowed by way of Preface:

1. The book is distinctly intended for learners, and not for doctors in Theology. It may be regarded as a first hand-book. If (as may be the case) I have erred in the way of simplicity and brevity, I shall, from my experience with those for whom the manual is primarily intended, count it an error on the right side.

2. References have generally been made to later rather than to older writers, because the former may more easily be consulted, and because for the most part they preserve and present the best of earlier thought, expressed in modern terms.

3. While it is hoped that an abundance of Scriptural passages have been cited or referred to, no attempt has been made to bring together all the passages connected with each point.

4. Two thoughts must continually be kept in mind: (a) Christian doctrine is largely, if not exclusively, concerned with truths that are revealed. We shall expect these to be above the reach of unaided reason; (b) Nevertheless reason will try to understand what is revealed.

5. Orthodox belief and religious living are closely connected. The one is to be a help to the other. We should build up our our own and one another's moral and spiritual life on the foundation of our most holy faith.

"The Incarnation opened Heaven, for it was the revelation of the Word; but it also reconsecrated earth, for the Word was made flesh, and dwelt among us."

A. C. A. H.

Epiphany, 1909.

THE CREEDS

THE APOSTLES' CREED

I BELIEVE

1. In God the Father Almighty,
   Maker of heaven and earth:

2. And in Jesus Christ his only Son our Lord:

3. Who was conceived by the Holy Ghost,
   Born of the Virgin Mary:

4. Suffered under Pontius Pilate,
   Was crucified, dead, and buried:

5. He descended into hell;
   The third day he rose again from the dead:

6. He ascended into heaven,
   And sitteth on the right hand of God the Father Almighty:

7. From thence he shall come to judge the quick and the dead.

8. I believe in the Holy Ghost:

9. The holy Catholic Church;
   The Communion of Saints:

10. The Forgiveness of Sins:

11. The Resurrection of the body:

12. And the Life everlasting.　　　　　Amen.

THE NICENE CREED

I BELIEVE

1. In one God the Father Almighty,
   Maker of heaven and earth,
   And of all things visible and invisible:

2. And in one Lord Jesus Christ, the only-begotten Son of God;
   Begotten of his Father before all worlds,
   God of God, Light of Light, Very God of very God;
   Begotten, not made;
   Being of one substance with the Father;
   By whom all things were made:

3. Who for us men and for our salvation came down from heaven,
   And was incarnate by the Holy Ghost of the Virgin Mary,
   And was made man:

4. And was crucified also for us under Pontius Pilate;
   He suffered and was buried:

5. And the third day he rose again according to the Scriptures:

6. And ascended into heaven,
   And sitteth on the right hand of the Father:

7. And he shall come again, with glory, to judge both the quick and the dead;
   Whose kingdom shall have no end.

8. And I believe in the Holy Ghost,
   The Lord, and Giver of Life,
   Who proceedeth from the Father and the Son;
   Who with the Father and the Son together is worshipped and glorified;
   Who spake by the Prophets:

9. And I believe one Catholic and Apostolic Church:

10. I acknowledge one Baptism for the remission of sins:

11. And I look for the Resurrection of the dead:

12. And the Life of the world to come.   Amen.

CREDO

1. *in Deum, Patrem Omnipotentem, Creatorem coeli et terrae.*
2. *Et in Jesum Christum Filium ejus unicum, Dominum nostrum:*
3. *qui conceptus est de Spiritu Sancto, natus ex Maria Virgine:*
4. *passus sub Pontio Pilato, crucifixus, mortuus, et sepultus:*
5. *descendit ad inferos; tertia die resurrexit a mortuis:*
6. *ascendit ad coelos, sedet ad dexteram Dei Patris omnipotentis:*
7. *inde venturus est judicare vivos et mortuos.*
8. *Credo in Spiritum Sanctum:*
9. *Sanctam Ecclesiam Catholicam; Sanctorum communionem:*
10. *remissionem peccatorum:*
11. *carnis resurrectionem:*
12. *vitam aeternam.*   *Amen.*

Πιστεύω

1. εἰς ἕνα Θεὸν Πατέρα παντοκράτορα, ποιητὴν οὐρανοῦ καὶ γῆς, ὁρατῶν τε πάντων καὶ ἀοράτων.

2. Καὶ εἰς ἕνα Κύριον Ἰησοῦν Χριστὸν, τὸν υἱὸν τοῦ Θεοῦ τὸν μονογενῆ, τὸν ἐκ τοῦ Πατρὸς γεννηθέντα πρὸ πάντων τῶν αἰώνων, φῶς ἐκ φωτός, θεὸν ἀληθινὸν ἐκ Θεοῦ ἀληθινοῦ, γεννηθέντα οὐ ποιηθέντα, ὁμοούσιον τῷ Πατρί· δι' οὗ τὰ πάντα ἐγένετο·

3. Τὸν δι' ἡμᾶς τοὺς ἀνθρώπους καὶ διὰ τὴν ἡμετέραν σωτηρίαν κατελθόντα ἐκ τῶν οὐρανῶν, καὶ σαρκωθέντα ἐκ Πνεύματος Ἁγίου καὶ Μαρίας τῆς παρθένου, καὶ ἐνανθρωπήσαντα·

4. Σταυρωθέντα τε ὑπὲρ ἡμῶν ἐπὶ Ποντίου Πιλάτου, καὶ παθόντα καὶ ταφέντα·

5. Καὶ ἀναστάντα τῇ τρίτῃ ἡμέρᾳ κατὰ τὰς γραφάς·

6. Καὶ ἀνελθόντα εἰς τοὺς οὐρανοὺς καὶ καθεζόμενον ἐκ δεξιῶν τοῦ Πατρὸς,

7. Καὶ πάλιν ἐρχόμενον μετὰ δόξης κρῖναι ζῶντας καὶ νεκρούς· οὗ τῆς βασιλείας οὐκ ἔσται τέλος.

8. Καὶ εἰς τὸ Πνεῦμα τὸ ἅγιον, τὸ κύριον καὶ τὸ ζωοποιόν, τὸ ἐκ τοῦ Πατρὸς ἐκπορευόμενον, τὸ σὺν Πατρὶ καὶ Ὑιῷ συμπροσκυνούμενον καὶ συνδοξαζόμενον, τὸ λαλῆσαν διὰ τῶν προφητῶν.

9. Εἰς μίαν ἁγίαν καθολικὴν καὶ ἀποστολικὴν ἐκκλησίαν·

10. Ὁμολογῶ ἓν βάπτισμα εἰς ἄφεσιν ἁμαρτιῶν·

11. Προσδοκῶ ἀνάστασιν νεκρῶν,

12. Καὶ ζωὴν τοῦ μέλλοντος αἰῶνος.   Ἀμήν.

NOTE.— The above is the Nicene Creed as said in the Greek liturgies, *i. e.* the Creed of Jerusalem, wlth the Nicene additions as ratified at Chalcedon.

CONTENTS

Chapter I.— Belief

The Nature of Faith — To believe a fact, to believe a person, to believe *in* a person — Grounds of belief: the revelation of God in nature, history, reason and conscience, the Prophets, Christ — The revelation in Christ final, but its significance continually unfolded — Formation of Creeds — They state facts not theories — Their relation to Scripture — Authority of the Church: That of a witness — Internal testimony — Moral character of faith — Faith and reason — Faith and theology — Theological dogmas — The order of belief.

Chapter II.— God the Creator

Belief in God — Natural arguments — Teaching of the Old Testament — Teaching of Christ and the Apostles — God is Spirit — Self-existent — Infinite — A person — Almighty — Omniscient. Rival Systems: Dualism — Monism (Materialism, Pantheism) — God's immanence and transcendence — Creation and Evolution — Man the crown of creation — The image of God — Rational, moral, immortal. Angels: their probation — The devil.

Chapter III.— God the Tri-une Being

The Unity of God more fundamental than the Trinity — Disclosure of the Trinity in the Baptismal commission — Picture at our Lord's Baptism — Teaching of His farewell discourse — Teaching of the

Apostles—The essential and the economic Trinity—
Analogies of the Trinity—The term 'Person' used
of the Trinity—The Monarchia—Subordination—
Hooker's summary—The *Quicunque vult*.

CHAPTER IV.—THE INCARNATION

The Incarnation the climax of God's self-manifestation—The four great doctrinal decisions concerning the Incarnation: (1) Christ was *truly* God—How the disciples came to this conviction; (2) He became *completely* man; (3) The human nature was *inseparably* linked with His divine person—The title θεοτόκος—The *communicatio idiomatum;* (4) The divine and human natures remained *unconfused*—Ubiquitarianism—The *Quicunque vult*.

CHAPTER V.—THE ATONEMENT

The Fall of Man—Transmission of disordered nature—The Atonement variously represented: (1) The manifestation of God's love; (2) The example of a perfect human life; (3) A moral victory over temptation; (4) A perfect satisfaction—meaning of propitiation; (5) All effected by Christ's Blood.

Symbolism of the Levitical sacrifices. Christ's sacrifice involves no division of attributes in the Trinity—He is our Representative not our Substitute—His obedience is His sacrifice—He died *by* sin, *for* sin, *to* sin.

CHAPTER VI.—THE RESURRECTION

Meaning of the Descent into Hades—The Vital and the Personal Union in Christ—His disembodied soul not inactive—The Resurrection a sign repeatedly promised—Continually pressed by the Apostles—

This involves a real resurrection. The Resurrection no return to former conditions — Difference between Christ's resurrection and such as had occurred before. The resurrection "according to the Scriptures." Purposes of the appearances after the resurrection. The Ascension the exaltation of our nature — Assurance of sympathy in Heaven — Christ present by His Spirit, though removed from sensible cognizance. The Return to judgment.

Chapter VII.—The Holy Ghost

Relation of the Spirit's work to that of Christ — The Giver of Life — The deity of the Holy Spirit — His distinct personality — His interior operation — "The Lord and the Life-giver" — "Who spake by the Prophets." The single or double Procession.

Grace the operation of the Spirit of God — requires our coöperation — not irresistible — the Paraclete.

Chapter VIII.—The Church

The Church corresponds with man's social being — Not a voluntary organization but a spiritual organism. Admission to the Church by Baptism (our promises and God's gift) — sealed in Confirmation — maintained in the Eucharist — The principle of Sacraments — This fellowship broken by sin — Spiritual discipline.

The Notes of the Church: (1) One, (2) Holy, (3) Catholic, (4) Apostolic — The transmission of the ministerial commission. Different organs of the body having each its appropriate function. The Catholic Church the elect body — Our individual share in the privileges of the Church: election, justification, sanctification, glorification.

Chapter IX.— Eschatology

Continued existence after death not a distinctive Christian doctrine — Sanctioned by Christ, with the added doctrine of the resurrection of the body. This not a return to former conditions of life — the spiritual body. The soul not unconscious in the intermediate state — The condition of the faithful departed one of progress, aided by prayers. Their future glory described under many allegorical figures, all summed up in perfect Life. The opposite of this is spiritual Death, likewise variously described — Irretrievable ruin a possibility — due to persistent rejection of God's purpose. This life the term of probation. Final reward or doom no arbitrary appointments, but the working out of the law of Retribution. Question as to the endless existence of the lost.

Appendices

A.— The Christian doctrine of God (James Orr).

B.— Creation and Evolution (G. H. Curteis).

C.— Possession by evil spirits (T. B. Strong).

D.— The Incarnation (W. Bright and B. F. Westcott).

E.— Scripture and Church Authority (S. Cyprian and Abp. Bramhall).

F.— Predestination and Election (C. Gore).

G.— Physical Death and its connection with sin (C. Gore).

H.— Eternal Life and its loss (W. E. Gladstone).

THE DOCTRINE OF THE CHURCH

I.

BELIEF

The Nature of Faith.— Belief primarily means intellectual assent, the acceptance of a statement as true on the authority of the speaker. In this sense belief may have varying degrees of certainty, corresponding with the authority of the speaker (his knowledge and his veracity). The acceptance of God's word will be absolute; our faith is unhesitating when once we are assured that a statement is from Him. Religious faith is a knowledge of spiritual facts, which could not be discovered with certainty by man's unaided reason, but which are revealed by God.

But Christian faith means more than mere intellectual assent. It stands for the acceptance by the whole man, in mind and heart and will, of the divine word, so that the man shall be moulded by the truth revealed. Further still, faith is specially used of a relation and attitude towards *a person*. In this sense it means not only belief that such an one exists, and belief that what he states is true, but also the trustful surrender of ourselves to the person in whom we believe (as a wife to her husband, a pupil to his master, soldiers to their leader). It is to faith of this kind directed towards God and our Lord Jesus Christ that the great promises in the New Testament are made,[1] *e. g.*:

"He that believeth in me, though he die, yet shall he live; and whosoever liveth and believeth in me shall never die." (John xi. 25, 26.)

"We believed in Jesus Christ, that we might be justified by faith in Christ." (Gal. ii. 16.)

It is this spiritual attitude of self-surrender which should be expressed by our profession of *belief in* God, in His incarnate Son, and in His Spirit. The Catechism thus rightly summarizes "what we chiefly learn" in the Articles of the Creed: We believe in God the Father who made us; in God the Son who redeemed us; and in God the Holy Ghost who sanctifies us. All the *truths* which we profess to *believe*, gather around the *persons* of the tri-une God, *in whom* we believe. These truths we unhesitatingly believe as facts — that all things in heaven and earth were made by God; that the incarnate Son was miraculously born in our nature, that He died and rose again, etc. We recognize the Church which the Spirit forms, the forgiveness of sins that He bestows, we look for the resurrection and the life of the world to come for which He prepares us. But all these truths we regard in their relation to the Father, the

---

[1] See Note C in the author's Bedell Lectures *The Relations of Faith and Life*, on the use of πιστεύειν in the New Testament with different prepositions and cases.

Son, and the Holy Spirit, as telling us about God and what He has done and does for us.[2]

For this entire acceptance of God's promised word and the surrender of ourselves to Him, we must seek and use the promised aid of the Spirit of God illuminating our intellectual and strengthening our moral faculties. Like all true knowledge, faith is appropriated and certified by experience, the experience of spiritual life. (See 2 Peter i. 5, John iv. 42, 2 Tim. i.12.)

Grounds of Belief.— God has made known to us in various ways, and in a progressive development, Himself, His working and His mind:

1. *Nature*, the work of His hands, gives a reflexion, however fragmentary, of the Creator. (Rom. i. 20, 21; Acts xiv. 17.)

2. *History* shows the working of His Providence gradually accomplishing His purposes, and making for the triumph of right.

3. The individual *Reason and Conscience* are enlightened by the Word of God. (John i. 9; Rom. ii.15.)

(The above belong to what is called Natural Religion, and are common to all men. Such knowledge of God as is thus given is presupposed in direct revelation.)

---

[2] Bishop Lightfoot says, " The phrase which occurs in the revised Nicene and other creeds, πιστεύειν εἰς ἐκκλησίαν, though an intelligible, is yet a lax expression, the propriety of which was rightly disputed by many of the fathers, who maintained that πιστεύειν εἰς should be reserved for belief in God or in Christ." (*Galatians* ii. 16, p. 115.)

4. He has from time to time raised up *prophets and teachers* to receive special revelations of His mind, and to declare to others what they have received. By the Prophets (in this wider sense of the word) He formed and trained Israel, His chosen people, in special preparation for the coming of His Son, whom they were taught to look for as the Messiah. (John iv. 22.)

5. Finally He sent *His incarnate Son*. "God, having of old time spoken unto the fathers in the prophets by divers portions and in divers manners, hath at the end of these days spoken unto us in his Son." (Heb. i. 1, 2.)

In Christ's life and teaching we have for this world a full and final revelation (1) of *God* — His being and character and purposes, and (2) of *man* — his origin and destiny, the true standard of his life, his relation to and means of approaching his Maker. This revelation, made once for all in and through Christ (Jude 3; Gal. i.8; 2 John 9), and recorded in the New Testament Scriptures, is continually unfolded and its bearings applied by the Holy Spirit, whom Christ sends to dwell in His Church. (John xiv. 26, xvi, 13.) The external testimony finds a response and sanction in the experience of the Church and of its individual members. But while the spiritual value of the truths gives to them a new force and justification, it must always be remembered that their value and significance depend upon the reality of the facts; and that the declarations of the Gospels or the Creeds are not mere symbols of subjective spiritual truths. The renewal of human nature, conquest of sin and death, union with God, are the great spiritual truths represented by the Incarnation, the Passion and Resurrection, and the Ascension of our Lord Jesus Christ. But these values in spiritual experience are made possible by the actual facts stated in the Creed.

What Christ and the Apostles in His name taught, that we accept without hesitation, as absolutely true. To this revelation the Christian Church bears constant testimony. Its leading truths are summed up in the Creeds.

Formation of Creeds.—The gradual formation of the Creeds we are able to trace as expansions of the Baptismal formula or charge in Matthew xxviii. 19.[3]

In Romans vi. 17, xii. 6, 1 Timothy vi. 20, 2 Timothy i. 13, Hebrews v. 12, x. 23, we have hints of a form of sound or healthful words, summarizing the great truths of the Christian religion, to be carefully guarded.[4]

Irenæus (A. D. 180) says that the Church, though dispersed throughout the whole world, has received

---

[3] On this passage and its authority see Dr. Sanday's article "God," in Hastings's *Dictionary of the Bible*, Vol. II. pp. 213, 214, and an article in *The Journal of Theological Studies* for September, 1905, on "The Lord's command to baptize," by Dr. Chase (now Bishop of Ely), who concludes an exhaustive examination of the question by saying, "The whole evidence— such I believe must be the verdict of scientific criticism—establishes without a shadow of doubt or uncertainty the genuineness of Matthew xxviii. 19."

[4] For a full discussion of the Creed see E. C. S. Gibson, *The Thirty-nine Articles*, Article VIII, and the same author's volume on *The Three Creeds* in the Oxford Library of Practical Theology.

from the Apostles and their disciples this faith: "In one God, the Father Almighty, Maker of heaven and earth and the sea, and all things that are in them; and in one Christ Jesus, the Son of God, who became incarnate for our salvation; and in the Holy Spirit, who proclaimed through the prophets the dispensations of God, and the advents, and the birth from a virgin, and the passion, and the resurrection from the dead, and the ascension into heaven, in the flesh, of the beloved Christ Jesus, our Lord, and His manifestation from heaven in the glory of the Father to gather all things in one, and to raise up anew all flesh of the whole human race." — (*Against Heresies*, bk. I, ch. x.)

What is called the Apostles' Creed represents in its main structure and contents the baptismal creed of all local churches, whether Eastern or Western, in early Christian times. Its particular form is that of the local church at Rome, the use of which, on account of the commanding position of the imperial city, naturally became more widely known in Western Christendom than that of other remote churches. We can trace it from the middle of the second century. The Creed was gradually expanded till it reached its present form in the seventh or eighth century, largely through the assimilation of articles of the baptismal confessions of other parts of Christendom.

The Nicene Creed is so called because (save some later additions) it was set forth at the council of Nicea (A. D. 325), to guard the truth of our Lord's Godhead, which was impugned by Arius. (See ch.

IV.) Later the third part of the Creed was developed, to guard the truth of the Godhead of the Holy Spirit. If this was not agreed upon by the Council of Constantinople (A. D. 381), the Creed in its full form was recognized by the Council of Chalcedon (A.D. 451).

The elaboration of the Creed (which will be illustrated by a comparison of the second article in the Apostles' Creed with the Nicene) was forced upon the Church by heretics rather than voluntarily undertaken. Fuller dogmatic statements were rendered necessary when the simple meaning of earlier statements was denied or explained away. The object of the Church was not to limit Christian thought, but rather to keep wide the region of truth in opposition to various heresies which attempted to contract it by denying one or other element thereof (for instance, either Christ's true Godhead or His real manhood). The Church's balanced statements are intended to preserve the full truth. In this way they guard freedom.

The Creeds state Facts not Theories.—It is further to be noted that the Creeds state facts not theories; we profess our belief in great truths revealed by Almighty God, not in explanations of those truths. No *doctrine* of the Trinity, as a method by which in thought we reconcile the truth of the absolute unity of God with His three-fold being, is propounded for our belief; nor any theory as to the manner in which the divine and human natures are united in the single person of our Lord Jesus Christ; nor any explanation of the way in which His death avails for our reconciliation with God. It is the same with reference to the exact limits or organization of the Christian Church, the way in which the inner grace is linked with the outward sign in sacraments, or the nature of the resurrection body. It is the fact, and not the explanation of the truth, which moulds the life, and which is *de fide*, important as an intelligent grasp of the truth must be. Here is the legitimate distinction between Faith and Theology.

Relation of Creeds to Scripture.—The Creeds summarize in a partially systematic order the chief truths taught in the Scriptures. Their statements may all be *proved* by Scripture, though in their earliest forms they existed before the New Testament Scriptures were written. The Church holds that it has been so ordered by God's Providence that all truths necessary for our spiritual life are contained in the Scriptures which the Church accepts as canonical. To these she appeals as a check upon human inventions, and particularly to the writings of apostles and apostolic men, as her purest tradition of the revelation given by Jesus Christ.

Authority.—The function of the Church is rather that of Witness than of Judge. The Church holds the records of those to whom the revelation was originally given. By their agreement or harmony with these records, and with the continuous tradition of the Church, opinions are tested. For its acceptance the opinion must be a legitimate explanation of a revealed truth, or a necessary deduction from it, the balancing force of other revealed truths being observed. No other kind of 'development' of Christian doctrine is warranted.

The general consent of the Church is understood to express the mind of the Spirit, who dwells in the faithful to lead them into all the truth.[5] Individual opinions are checked and balanced by the evidence of fellow-members of the body. This is the principle of the Church's authority in matters of faith.

The authority of the Church does not supersede, but influences and guides our own individual judgment. The external witness of the Church is of the nature of evidence, expert evidence we might say, appealing to our judgment. With the external testimony should correspond the internal evidence of our moral sense and of our affections. God makes His appeal to the whole man. It is for this reason, in part, that faith is counted of such great importance in the New Testament. Acceptance or rejection of the divine message, when fairly brought before a man, is,

---

[5] On the ultimate appeal in matters of faith to Scripture, and to Scripture as interpreted by the Catholic Church, and in subordination to this supreme authority to the decisions of a national Church, see (for the Fathers) S. Cyprian and (for Anglican divines) Abp. Bramhall, quoted in Appendix E.

See also Article VI, "Of the Sufficiency of the Holy Scriptures for Salvation," XX "Of the Authority of the Church," and XXI "Of the Authority of General Councils," and Gibson's comments thereon. We use tradition as a help towards arriving at the true sense of Scripture, not as an additional source of Christian doctrine. The same Convocation which in 1571 imposed subscription to the Thirty-nine Articles on the English clergy, required preachers to take care that they never preach aught to be religiously held and believed by the people, except what is agreeable to the doctrine of the Old and New Testaments, and what the Catholic fathers and ancient bishops have collected from the same doctrine.—(Cardwell, *Synodalia*, I. p. 126.)

in general, a test of his character, of those moral qualities which must affect the intellectual judgment, his sincerity and purity of heart, his obedience, his correspondence with previous opportunities.[6]

He that hath to him shall be given.

Blessed are the pure in heart, for they shall see God.

He that willeth to do His will, he shall know of the teaching whether it be of God.

He that is of God heareth God's words. (Mark iv. 25; Matt. v. 8; John vii. 17, viii. 47.)

Faith and Reason.—That which is proposed for acceptance by faith must never be contrary to reason. Faith lays hold on truths made known to us, which by our unaided powers we could not have discovered, or at which we should only have guessed as probable. But we can only employ for the reception of truth the faculties with which God has endowed us. Faith is no additional faculty. It is reason illuminated by the Spirit of God. A new *power* is given by grace to the existing natural *faculty*. If we were asked, on whatever authority, to believe something that is contrary to our reason, we should be obliged to refuse. Faith may go beyond our experience; it is above reason; but it can never contradict the verdict of our senses, our reason, or our conscience.

Faith and Theology.—The great facts of our religion are unchangeable. The faith of the Church concerning their substance is unalterable. But explana-

---

[6] See the second of the author's Bedell Lectures, "The Effect of Life on Faith."

tions of the truth will vary with stages and phases of human development—development of the race as of the individual. As the truth is expressed in the language of each nation, so it must of necessity be conceived and expressed in harmony with the thought and philosophy of the age. Thus the theology, the systematic and philosophical presentation of the Church's faith, may show a variation between the first, the fourth, the sixteenth and the twentieth centuries. The *same truth,* e. g. of the Trinity, or the Redemption, or the Sacraments, or the future life, will be somewhat *differently apprehended and explained* at different periods. The definitions of a later age must not contradict nor be at variance with those already accepted by the Church, though it is conceivable that the same truth might be expressed in other words.

Theological Dogmas.—Scientific theology is not merely a systematic exhibition of what we believe; it aims at showing the reasonableness of our belief. As systematic it must necessarily be dogmatic. "Dogma is definition, nothing more. It presupposes that we know certain truths not alone with the certitude of spiritual experience, but according to the categories of the intellect. If we know nothing, we cannot dogmatize; if we know anything with certainty, we must dogmatize. It is to be regretted that the word dogma has been appropriated so exclusively to the formulating of religious truth, for this obscures the identity of the process with clearness of definition in all branches of knowledge. There are dogmas of science, dogmas of philosophy, dogmas of trade, just as truly as there are dogmas of religion. The difference of subject matter and methods of arriving at conclusions ought not to blind us to this obvious fact."—(W. L. Robbins, *An Essay toward Faith*, p. 156.)

Order of Belief.—The order of belief, *i. e.* the process by which persons come to an acknowledgment of the Christian faith, may vary. Many persons may be first impressed by the life and teaching of Jesus Christ. Accepting Him as Master, they recognize that He made claims altogether inconsistent with moral excellence in a created being; the doctrine of the Trinity comes to them as a welcome explanation of what would otherwise be a hopeless puzzle. They come to believe in a personal God through belief in Jesus. But all the while there has been in the background of their mind an idea of God, which is now called forth and clarified. In an exposition of Christian doctrine it will be best to follow the logical order, to which all must ultimately come for an intelligent apprehension of the faith, by whatever truth they may have been first attracted.

BIBLIOGRAPHY

F. Temple, "The Relation between Religion and Science." (Bampton Lectures, 1884.)

P. N. Waggett, "The Scientific Temper in Religion."

P. N. Waggett, "Religion and Science." (Hand books for the Clergy.)

J. R. Illingworth, "Reason and Revelation."

B. F. Westcott, "The Historic Faith," cc. I and II.

W. L. Robbins, "An Essay toward Faith."

W. L. Robbins, "Apologetics." (Hand books for the Clergy.)
A. C. A. Hall, "Relations of Faith and Life." (Bedell Lectures.)
V. H. Stanton, "The Place of Authority in Matters of Religious Belief."
T. B. Strong, "Authority in the Church." (Hand books for the Clergy.)
T. B. Strong, "God and the Individual."
I. A. Dorner, "A System of Christian Doctrine," Introduction. (Clark's Foreign Theological Library.)
H. Martensen, "Christian Dogmatics," Introduction.
Harnack, "History of Dogma."
J. H. Skrine, "What is Faith?"
J. F. Bethune-Baker, "Introduction to the Early History of Christian Doctrine."
T. B. Strong, "A Manual of Theology."
A. J. Mason, "The Faith of the Gospel."
F. J. Hall, "Authority, Ecclesiastical and Biblical."

D. Stone, "Outlines of Christian Dogma."
T. A. Lacey, "The Elements of Christian Doctrine."
A. E. Burn, "An Introduction to the Creeds."
H. B. Swete, "The Apostles' Creed."
E. C. S. Gibson, "The Three Creeds." (Oxford Library of Practical Theology.)
C. A. Heurtley, "*De Fide et Symbolo*."
C. A. Swainson, "The Nicene and Apostles' Creeds."
J. Pearson, "Exposition of the Creed."
J. Lias, "The Nicene Creed."
T. H. Bindley, "The Oscumenical Documents of the Faith."
E. C. S. Gibson, "The Thirty-nine Articles."
B. J. Kidd, "The Thirty-nine Articles."
J. H. Newman, "The Grammar of Assent."

II.

GOD THE CREATOR

Belief in God.—The first article of our Creed, "I believe in God the Father Almighty, Maker of heaven and earth," means this at any rate, whatever more it means :

We acknowledge one supreme Being, in whom we, and all things, live and move and have our being; a spiritual Person, having powers of thought and affection and freedom of action, such as we associate with our minds and hearts and wills, and of which our powers of thought and feeling and choice are a reflection; 'the living God,' who intervenes and rules and judges in the affairs of men; a moral Being, whose action is characterised not merely by almighty power but also by infinite wisdom and perfect goodness.

How do we reach this belief? As Christians we believe in God because we are taught of Him by Jesus Christ. Our Lord did not teach a systematic theology. He assumed the existence of God, and to a large extent a knowledge of His character. This had been partially given in previous revelations; to all men in Nature, History, Reason and Conscience; to the Jews by special teachers, called Prophets, raised up from time to time to declare to others what God had taught them concerning Himself. Through these prophets Israel was made "a sacred school of religious knowledge for all mankind." — (Athanasius, *de Incarnatione*, xii.)

The existing conceptions of God Christ corrected when necessary and supplemented, telling us more about His character, and by implication, at any rate, about His being.

Natural Arguments. — Behind the direct revelation there was and is a natural conception of God, imperfect, often faulty, sometimes perverted, which is partly derived by tradition from an original revelation, such as primitive man was fitted to receive, party derived from man's own thought. The idea of God is always and everywhere a growing idea. Man's first conceptions of God are extremely anthropomorphic; the gods of Egypt were magnified human beings. As man advances in intelligence, and culture his conception of God is necessarily elevated.[1]

The lines of thought by which, apart from direct revelation, we arrive at the idea of God may be grouped under the following heads, which are placed not in their philosophical sequence, but rather in the actual order in which the arguments commonly present themselves. The words of John Stuart Mill may here be quoted: "The sender of the alleged message is not a sheer invention. There are grounds independent of the message itself for belief in his reality — grounds which, though insufficient for proof, are sufficient to take away all antecedent improbability from

---

[1] For a concise description of the primitive ideas of God, see Andrew Lang, *Myth, Ritual and Religion*.

the supposition that a message may really have been received from him."[2]

1. *Cosmological.*—This is an *a posteriori* argument, from what we observe in Nature. (Comp. Rom. i. 20, Ps. xix. 1.) The mind is so made that it demands a cause for every effect. We trace back all that we perceive to some First Cause, which must of necessity be self-existing. As no cause can impart what it has not in itself, we gather that the First Cause must be personal. (Ps. xciv. 9.) We are thus led to the recognition of a self-existent fashioner of the universe.

2. *Teleological.*—Correspondences and adjustments in the world show design. The gradual working out of a design through many stages of development heightens rather than otherwise the force of this consideration. The adaptation of means to ends points to the First Cause as an intelligent and intellectually powerful being. If some imaginable universe might have existed without a Creator, we feel that the universe with which we are acquainted could not.

3. *Moral.*—Our consciousness of right and wrong, of approval and disapproval, suggests an authority independent of and above men, to whom we are responsible. (Comp. Rom. ii. 15.) All phenomena must be taken into account, phenomena of the moral world not less than facts of the physical world.

4. *Ontological.*—An *a priori* argument, resting on the idea of pure being. That which is conceived in the mind must have an objective reality.

---

[2] From his posthumously published essay, "On Theism," part IV. p. 213, of essays on religion.

5. *Historical.*— From the common consent of mankind we see that human nature is so constituted that the belief in God instinctively commends itself to men.

These are not merely parallel or disconnected arguments; they are complementary and converging.

Teaching of the Old Testament.— Among the covenant people (Rom. ix. 4) man's thought is taken up and purified by progressive revelations, to the Patriarchs, in the Law and by the Prophets.

These are the truths about God which stand out most clearly in the Old Testament Scriptures:

1. *His sole Sovereignty.*— Hear, O Israel: the LORD our God is one LORD: and thou shalt love the LORD thy God with all thine heart, and with all thy soul and with all thy might. (Deut. vi. 4, 5. Comp. Isa. xliv. 6-8.)

2. *His Self-existence.*— God said unto Moses, I I AM THAT I AM: and he said, Thus shalt thou say unto the children of Israel, I AM hath sent me unto you. (Ex. iii. 14.)

3. *His inscrutable being.*— Canst thou by searching find out God?

Canst thou find out the Almighty unto perfection?
It is high as heaven; what canst thou do?
Deeper than Sheol; what canst thou know? (Job xi. 7, 8.)

4. *His Omniscience.*— I have declared the former things from of old; yea, they went forth out of my mouth, and I shewed them: suddenly I did them,

and they came to pass. . . . I have declared it to thee from of old; before it came to pass, I shewed it to thee. (Isa. xlviii. 3, 5; Comp. Ps. cxxxix. 1-18.)

5. *His Omnipotence.*— It is he that sitteth above the circle of the earth, and the inhabitants thereof are as grasshoppers; that stretcheth out the heavens as a curtain, and spreadeth them out as a tent to dwell in; that bringeth princes to nothing; that maketh the judges of the earth as vanity, etc. (Isa. xl. 22-26. Comp. xliv. 24-28.)

6. *His Righteousness.*— A God of faithfulness and without iniquity,

Just and right is he. (Deut. xxxii. 4).

The LORD, the LORD God, merciful and gracious, longsuffering, and abundant in goodness and truth, keeping mercy for thousands, forgiving iniquity and transgression and sin, and that will by no means clear *the guilty*. (Ex. xxxiv. 6, 7. Comp. Isa. vi. 1-5.)

Teaching of Christ.— This thought of God, developed among the Jews, especially on the side of His moral character, is sanctioned and emphasized by Jesus Christ. Christ's own teaching is mostly indirect. He makes God known as His Father, whose character He represents. Accordingly in the writings of the apostles, God is continually spoken of as "the Father of our Lord Jesus Christ." Jesus acts in His name, as He would act. As the incarnate Word He translates God's character into language of human conduct. God's holiness is understood in the purity of Jesus; God's love in the self-sacrifice of

Jesus; God's justice in His discrimination and consideration.

The following points stand out conspicuously in Christ's teaching about God, following upon and expanding the earlier Jewish doctrine:

1. His absolutely spiritual being (John iv. 24).

2. His righteousness is manifested especially in love, without any obscuring of His hatred of evil.

3. His care for *individuals*, while the stress before had been upon the nation of Israel. He is continually spoken of as "our heavenly Father" (*e. g.* Matt. vi).

4. His care for *all nations*, and not only for Israel.

Teaching of the Apostles.—It would be a useful practice to gather from the teaching of the apostles points in the doctrine about God that are insisted on. The following are only hints:

His spiritual being inaccessible in Himself (1 Tim. i. 7, vi. 15, 16, Acts vii. 48, xvii. 24);

His inscrutable and manifold wisdom (Rom. xi. *fin.*, Eph. iii. 10);

He is absolutely one, and consequently cares for all, and requires undivided devotion (1 Tim. ii. 4, 5, Rom. iii. 29, 1 Cor. viii. 4);

the Creator of all (Acts xiv. 15-17, xviii. 24, Heb. iii. 4, iv. 4),

and Judge (Acts xvii. 31, Rom. ii. 5),

knowing the hearts (Acts xv. 8, Heb. iv. 13);

Eternal (2 Pet. iii. 8);

Omniscient (Acts ii. 23, iii. 18);

Omnipotent (Eph. iv. 20);
the Source of all good (Jas. i. 17);
absolutely Holy (Jas. i. 13);
requiring holiness (Heb. ii. 14, 1 Pet. i. 17);
our Saviour (Tit. ii. 10).

Attributes of God.— Such descriptions lead to a consideration of the attributes of God. By these we mean what is attributed or ascribed to God, corresponding with what in man we call faculties or qualities. These are not constituent elements of the divine being, but rather activities or characteristics thereof. The attributes of God are sometimes classed as:

1. Absolute — His infinity, eternity, blessedness;
2. Relative — His omnipresence, omniscience, etc.;
3. Moral — His holiness, truth, love, etc.

About some of these descriptions or attributes a few words may be said by way of guarding against misunderstanding:

1. "God is *Spirit*," not *a* spirit, as if he were one among many. But this is His nature. (John iv. 24, Deut. iv. 15; Isa. xl. 18, 25.) "Without body, parts or passions."

For the sake of vivid presentment God is often spoken of in material terms. This is an instance of the common representation of spiritual realities under figures drawn from material existence. We ought always to consider what the figure stands for.

"When the Old Testament speaks of the hand, arm, mouth, lips, and eyes of God; when He makes bare His holy arm (Isa. lii. 10); lifts up a signal to the nations (xlix. 22); is seen at the head of the Medes mustering His hosts, and His military shout is heard (xiii. 4); all this is but the vivid conception of His being, His intelligence, His activity and universal power over the nations whom He directs."—(A. B. Davidson, in Hastings's *Dictionary of the Bible*, II. p. 198.)

Man is made in God's image; that is, our spiritual being, with its powers of reason and affection and choice, is a created and imperfect resemblance of God's uncreated being, intelligent, loving, free. All the emotions of which men are conscious, and all the human conduct corresponding to these emotions, are thrown back upon God. Impassible is not the same as unfeeling. Our changing moods and feelings are a reflection of the steady and unalterable regard with which a perfect moral being must view the correspondence (or lack thereof) with His will in things and persons. God is not a magnified man, but man's nature does reflect God's. "If anthropomorphism as applied to God is false, if God does not exist in man's image, yet theomorphism, as applied to man, is true; man is made in God's image, and his qualities are, not the measure of the divine, but their counterpart and real expression."—(Gore, Bampton Lectures, p. 125.)

2. God is *self-existent*. (a) This is probably the meaning of the name "Jehovah," or more properly "Yahweh" (Ex. iii. 14, 15, vi. 2, 3). (b) The idea is involved in that of a First Cause, to which all

else that exists may be traced back, through whatever process of origination. (c) It is this which distinguishes God from all created beings. Whatever gifts or powers they have, of whatever kind, they received them from Him. He is the one being who has everything and has received nothing.

3. God is *infinite*. (a) When we speak of God as infinite we must guard against a misconception which is really a denial of the true meaning of the word. The infinite is not that which is extended through all space, but that which exists independently of space, which includes all space within its own boundless existence. In the same way *eternal* is not equivalent to indefinite duration through all time. The eternal is that which is not only through or before or beyond, but above all time, to which the limits of time do not apply. The infinite God is equally present to the smallest and the largest of created things. He is not like an earthly monarch concerned only with general laws, while leaving to subordinate officers all details of execution and administration. Not a sparrow falls to the ground without our heavenly Father's knowledge. The hairs of our head are all numbered (Matt. x. 29, 30). (b) We must also observe that there is a self-limitation of God involved in the very act of creation. He calls into existence something which is not Himself. He is, in a sense, limited by the existence of this with Himself.

4. God is a *person*.— Powers of consciousness and choice which are found in man can be only the reflexion of corresponding features of the divine being.

(Dan. iv. 17, Eph. i. 11.) (See the Cosmological argument, p. 34.)

Because God is thus personal, "the living God," and no mere Soul of the Universe, we can reasonably approach Him in prayer, (1) both assured that He has a care and interest in our concerns, and (2) that He will respond to our petitions in whatever way His wisdom and love see best. God is not bound by laws of nature as if they existed independently of Himself, or as if He had once for all laid them down and was subject in His action to their regulation. The laws of the universe express our observation of the regularity of God's working, always in the best way (not in any tentative fashion), and therefore ordinarily in the same way. We shall expect that His action will be in accordance with His ordinary method, and not after any arbitrary fashion. But having all the forces of the universe at His disposal, He can apply them so as to serve His purposes and His people's needs.

5. God is *almighty*. When we say that God is almighty we do not mean that He can do *anything*, but that He is restrained by no *external* law. This is more exactly the sense of παντοκράτωρ, the Sovereign Ruler, which is the original of our 'Almighty' in the Creeds. God is free to do what He wills, but He cannot will that which would contradict the law of His own being — His truth, love, holiness. Nor will He contravene the freedom of choice with which He has endowed His moral creatures. By bestowing on them the prerogative of free-will, He has voluntarily limited His own action. In this way God tolerates the presence of evil in the world, while He limits its

operation and overrules it for ultimate and highest good. The devil is no second god or principle of being, but merely a rebel creature, who has abused the free-will with which God endowed him.

6. God is *omniscient*. A difficulty is sometimes felt in reconciling man's freedom of choice (a fact of which we are experimentally certain) with God's omniscience or foreknowledge (which is a necessary element of His infinite and eternal being). The difficulty is in great measure overcome by the consideration that while God's knowledge goes before men's actions in the order of time, it does not go before them in the order of causation. God sees our actions because we perform them (all things being present to Him); we do not perform them because He sees them, any more than seeing a distant object through a telescope, or a minute object through a microscope, causes the presence of the object. We see it with the aid of the glass, because it is there, though indistinguishable by our limited and unaided vision.

Rival Systems.— Over against the belief and teaching of the Church concerning God are two rival systems of thought. (Polytheism, though widely spread, need scarcely be taken into account as a third, since, wherever any intelligent statement of it is attempted, it is seen to recognize, in the background of its many gods, one supreme deity, whether personal or impersonal.)

1. *Dualism*, which asserts the existence of two first principles, one good and the other evil, the latter being often identified with matter.

2. *Monism*, the converse of Dualism, which asserts that evil does not really exist, but is only a lesser degree of goodness, and denies the distinction between matter and spirit, taking either the form (a) of *Materialism*, which denies all spiritual existence, or (b) of *Pantheism*, which regards all created things as being in truth a part of the divine nature. (On the Christian doctrine of God as embracing the elements of truth in different antagonistic systems, see Orr, quoted in Appendix A.)

In connection with Creation two questions present themselves to thinking persons at the present day: the question of God's Immanence and the question of Evolution. It should be said that neither of them is a new thought. Both have been in the minds of theologians from early times. In systems of Theology recently popular, both were doubtless largely ignored. Both have been brought to the fore of late.

I. *God's Immanence and Transcendence.*— There is no real question in the Church's mind between God's Immanence and His Transcendence, as if they were mutually exclusive. Both are true. They are different and supplementary aspects of the truth. If we have a right idea of God's *infinite* being (*immensus* is the Latin word for 'incomprehensible' in the Athanasian hymn), we shall recognize that all created beings, personal and impersonal, exist within His boundless being. He is not a distant God, immeasurably removed from the world. "In Him we live and move and have our being." (Acts xvii. 28. Comp. Ps. civ. 29, 30.) Nor again was anything once called into existence by God's *fiat*, and thereafter left to itself until the powers communicated wore themselves out. God is the Creator and Preserver of all. Moment by moment He upholds that which He has called into being. In Him all things consist and hold together. (Col. i. 17; Heb. i. 3; John v. 17.) And by all things we mean each in particular. While this is most certainly true, and there can only have been a lack of realization, and not a denial, of the truth in people's minds, it is also most certainly true that in every respect the Infinite transcends the finite. Creation is not co-extensive with the Creator. (Eph. iv. 6.) Heaven and earth are full of His glory; but they do not comprise His perfections. We shall recognize this perhaps most clearly in considering the moral being of God. If He were only immanent and not transcendent, there could be no higher manifestation of His holiness, no truer ideal, than the imperfect sanctity of His servants. Immanence, so far as it is opposed to transcendence, means that God is expressed, and only expressed, in the world.[3]

Such a doctrine, that God is the universal being of whose substance we all form a part, not only obscures the personal being of God and His holiness; but it

---

[3] The following quotations from *The New Theology*, by R. J. Campbell (given by Bishop Gore in his volume, *The New Theology and the Old Religion*, p. 43), illustrate this position: "God is the mysterious power which is finding expression in the universe and which is present in every tiniest atom of the wondrous whole. I find that this power is the only reality I cannot get away from; for, whatever else it may be, it is myself." — (*The New Theology*, p. 35.) "The real God is the God expressed in the universe, and in yourself."—(Ibid. p. 10.) "There is no dividing line between God's being, and ours."—(Ibid. p. 34.)

also tends to obliterate the reality of sin, and any true responsibility in man, for his real personality is lost in the ocean of life, of which he is merely a bubble on the surface. Against such vague notions, a recrudescence, it should be remembered, of Pagan ideas which the Christian religion conquered, the Christian creed utters its emphatic protest when it tells of God the Creator, the Redeemer and Restorer, the Judge of all. Christian doctrine should guard against both errors, the immersion of God in nature, and the isolation of nature from God.—(P. N. Waggett, *Religion and Science*, p. 110.)

II. *Creation and Evolution.*—The question between Evolution and Special Creation is not like that of the Immanence and the Transcendence of God. The latter, as we have seen, presents no real contrast. The two thoughts are supplementary the one to the other. On the other hand, Evolution or Development is contrasted with Special Creation. But, (it is to be remembered), the contrast is only between different processes of Creation. "If we believe, as we have seen that Christian Theology has always believed, in a Divine Creator not only present behind the beginning of matter but immanent in its every phase, and coöperating with its every phenomenon, the method of His working, though full of speculative interest, will be of no controversial importance."—(J. R. Illingworth, in *Lux Mundi*, p. 142.)

The theory of evolution is in no sense a denial of Creation. It helps us to understand more of the way in which the world was fashioned, emphasizing the patience, as well as the wisdom, of the Creator, gradually leading on His work to higher stages, with marvellous adaptation and a steady progress towards a perfect end. We see Him rendering each of the things of His Creation "at once a revelation and a prophecy, a thing of beauty and finished workmanship, worthy to exist for its own sake, and yet a step to higher purposes, an instrument for grander work." — (J. R. Illingworth, in *Lux Mundi*, p. 139.)

Evolution in the physical order corresponds with what we recognize to be the general method of God's dealing in the social order, and in our individual life. We see the development of institutions, or advance in character, (a) by stages, (b) working towards a perfect end, (c) with adaptation to circumstances, (d) through the coöperation of agencies and instrumentalities.

Man the Crown of Creation.— Evolution, like Holy Scripture, makes man the crown of creation in this world. At the base of the scale is inorganic matter; then we rise to organic life in the vegetable world; then comes animal and sentient life through insect, fish, reptile, bird and mammal, till we reach man. In him we find a self-conscious, personal, rational, moral being. This is the teaching alike of Evolution and of Scripture. Man is the crown and masterpiece of the whole edifice of creation. Nothing higher than man is looked for. Development is now *within* humanity, in man's rising to his best, and specially in *moral* progress.

As regards his lower nature it matters little for religious purposes whether we regard man as created immediately out of the dust of the ground, or whether we suppose that many stages intervened through which the dust of the ground (his ultimate material origin) was gradually fashioned into the form of man. At a particular point God bestowed upon man a distinct gift of life beyond that which came (directly or indirectly) from the dust of the ground. In both accounts of the Creation (Gen. i. and ii.), while man is represented as sharing the nature of the world around him, he is spoken of as having a unique nature, made "in the image of God," with reference to his mental and moral faculties.

Man made in the image of God.—The image of God in which man is made consists, (1) in his *rational* being; he can understand the world that God has made. Reason in man and the reason expressed in nature must be the same in kind, or there could be no relation between them; (2) in his *moral* being. He recognizes duty, distinguishes between good and evil, right and wrong. He can choose, and within limitations is self-determining. It is the power of will and self-determination which most of all constitute man's *personal* being.

These faculties of reason, affection, conscience and will belong to man by nature. The higher activities of the soul we designate spiritual, as distinct from the vital functions of the body, with its appetites, desires and impulses. By the exercise of these higher faculties man is capable of entering into spiritual relations with his invisible Creator.

Man is a created image of God in his being and faculties, and is intended to reflect the moral character of God. Possessing faculties which make him resemble God, he is to use them so that his action resembles God's. In God the perfect harmony of His power and wisdom and goodness constitute His holiness (almighty power always exercised in accordance with infinite wisdom and in perfect love). So it is with holiness in man.

In the right exercise of his power of choice consists man's goodness; by its misuse he falls away from God and from his own true dignity.

These natural powers of man being so great it is generally believed that immortality is a part of the image of God in which man is made; that this too is a part of man's natural endowment, rather than a superadded gift of grace. But this opinion cannot be regarded as a matter of faith, and it is disputed by many.[4] Where it is held, the distinction must be carefully noted between this *endlessness of existence*, the indestructibility of the frame of his spiritual being, and the *eternal life* which is the reward of those who have with God's aid cultivated and exercised aright their natural capacities. Of this eternal life *spiritual death* is the counterpart, by which is meant, not annihilation, but the waste and wreck, through misuse, of capacities and powers that must continue to exist, though in a ruined condition.

The Angels.— Man is not the only intelligent creature that God has made. As beneath him are

---

[4] See W. E. Gladstone, "Studies subsidiary to the works of Bishop Butler."

lower creatures that share his physical, but not his spiritual, being; so we are taught in Holy Scripture that there are higher intelligences which share his spiritual, but not his physical, being. These spiritual intelligences are called Angels, and apparently are of many ranks. (Eph. i. 21; Col. i. 16; 1 Pet. iii. 22.)

The angels, like man, were created upright; but as they were moral beings like him must pass through probation, and exercise their power of choice. Some fell and became fixed in evil, their spiritual being with its clearer vision rendering their fall irreparable. Of the evil or fallen angels the devil or Satan is the leader, and exerts the powers bestowed on him by God for His service, in antagonism to His purposes and for the seduction and ruin of His creature man. (Mk. iv, 15; John viii, 44; Eph. vi, 12; 1 Peter v, 8; Jude 6; 1 John iii, 8; Rev. xii, 9.)[5]

---

[5] Concerning Angels, good and evil, see Gore's *Dissertations*, pp. 21-27, Lect. II. of the author's Baldwin Lectures, *Christ's Temptation and Ours*, and the article "Angels" in Hastings's *Dictionary of the Bible* by A. B. Davidson, as well as the quotation from T. B. Strong in Appendix C.

BIBLIOGRAPHY

J. R. Illingworth, "Personality, Human and Divine." (Bampton Lectures, 1894.)

J. R. Illingworth, "The Divine Immanence."

Aubrey Moore, "The Christian Doctrine of God," in *Lux Mundi*.

F. J. Hall, "The Doctrine of God."

James Orr, "The Christian View of God and the World," Lectures III, IV, V.

"C. E. D'Arcy, "Christianity and the Supernatural" (Anglican Church Handbooks), a modern plea for the place of Transcendence.

C. E. Luthardt, "Fundamental Truths of Christianity."

H. Lotze, "Microcosmus," bk. VII. and bk. IX. cc. 4 and 5.

H. T. S. Eck, "Sin" (Oxford Library of Practical Theology).

W. H. Hutchings, "The Mystery of the Temptation," Lecture III.

E. H. Jewett, "Diabolology."

W. Knight, "Aspects of Theism."

Robert Flint, "Theism."

E. Griffith-Jones, "Ascent through Christ."

The editor would also call attention to the essay entitled "Angels" in Dr. Sanday's "Life of Christ in recent research."

References to a more thorough study of the reasons for belief in God will be found in the volume upon Apologetics in this series.

III.

GOD THE TRI-UNE BEING

The Unity of God more fundamental than the Trinity.— In order to think rightly — or not of necessity to think wrongly — concerning the doctrine of the Trinity, we must be quite clear about the absolute and indissoluble *Unity of God.* This is a more fundamental truth than that of the Trinity. It was not until this belief had been firmly impressed upon the Jewish people, by all the teaching and experience of the Old Testament, that God ventured to disclose the further truth of the Trinity; that within the absolute and indissoluble oneness of the Supreme Being there is a distinction which, for lack of better terminology, we speak of as a distinction of Persons; the Father, the Son, and the Holy Spirit. Uninstructed people are apt to begin with the thought of the three Persons, and then work back to the one nature common to the three, in the same way that we think of three individual men sharing a common human nature. But with God we must begin with the thought of His oneness, and then within that oneness we are taught to recognize a three-fold mode of being.

It has been pointed out that the very titles by which the three Persons of the Trinity are known to us imply the unity of their life. "They are not proper names, like those of heathen divinities, but titles of relationship, which involve each other, and would be meaningless alone. Fatherhood is impossible without sonship, and sonship without fatherhood; a spirit (in the sense in which the word is applied to the Holy Ghost) is impossible without one whose spirit it is."—(Mason, *Faith of the Gospel*, p. 48.)

The disclosure of the Trinity in the New Testament is made most clearly by our Lord in the great commission delivered shortly before His ascension: "Go, and make disciples of all the nations, baptizing them into the name of the Father and of the Son and of the Holy Ghost." (Matt. xxviii. 19.) Here our Lord is giving a summary of that which is to be taught: disciples are to be won to acknowledgment of the Father, the Son, and the Holy Spirit. The first and second of these titles are evidently personal; the third must be, likewise. The joining in this connection of the name of the Supreme God with that of a created representative and of a divine influence would be inconceivable. Moreover, "the name" is distinctly singular; it is the one name of God, who is Father, Son, and Holy Spirit. This is His name (we may say) fully written out, whereby Christians are to know Him, as in former times He was made known to His covenant people as God Almighty, the God of their fathers, I AM, the Self-existent One, the Holy One of Israel, the Lord of hosts. (Ex. iii. 13-16, iv. 2, 3; 2 Kgs. xix. 22; Isa. i. 4, v. 24.) Into this Name Christians are baptized into acknowledgment of, surrender to, and fellowship with God so described.

Our Lord's baptismal commission in the name of the Tri-une God is illustrated by the vision of the

GOD THE TRI-UNE BEING

Trinity vouchsafed at His own Baptism, which stands near the beginning of each of the Synoptic Gospels. (Matt. iii. 16, 17; Mark i, 10, 11; Luke iii. 21, 22.) The voice of the Father was heard testifying to the beloved Son, upon whom the Spirit was seen descending. This picture of the Trinity forms a sort of frontispiece to the Gospel, giving an illustration of what will be explained in our Lord's teaching that follows. The voice speaking in conscience and nature and history, which from its authority we recognize as coming from heaven, is interpreted to us as the voice of the Father, who is made known to us in His Son manifest in human form; on the Son in our nature descends and rests the Spirit of God to hallow Him and fit Him for His work. As we are united to Christ by faith and obedience, and through the sacraments which He ordains for this purpose, so we are accepted by God in Him the well-beloved Son, and God's Spirit is imparted to us as Christ's members. What was externally represented in objective vision at Christ's Baptism is in the spiritual sphere continually realised in the administration of Christian Baptism. In the strength of this vision we are to go forth, as did Christ, to meet temptation, to accomplish our work, to bear suffering. The representation of the Trinity at the beginning of the Gospel and the commission to baptize in the name of the Trinity at its close, should be taken together as illustrating one another, and as showing the meaning of intermediate teaching during the Lord's ministry. Especially prominent in this respect is the last discourse (John xiv.-xvi.), in which our Lord prepared His disciples for His departure and promised another Helper in His place.

In this farewell address —

(1) Jesus declares, "He that hath seen me hath seen the Father" (xiv. 9), which cannot be explained save by the recognition of Him as really the incarnate Son of God, of one nature with the Father and manifest in our nature.

(2) He speaks of the Spirit as taking His place (xiv. 16), which would be impossible unless the Spirit were a personal being like Himself, and equally with Himself (though in a different manner) representative of the Father, and proceeding from Him.

(3) Personal distinctions are clearly implied in the words, "I will pray the Father, and He shall give you another Comforter" (xiv. 16). The Son prays; the Father hears and gives; the Spirit comes.

(4) A real equality is implied in the promises, "I will come unto you," and "We will come unto you" (xiv. 18, 23).

(5) These same promises (that the Father will send the Spirit in Christ's name, that Christ will send the Spirit from the Father) point to the unbroken unity of the Godhead, the real oneness of the Tri-une Being.

"He [the Spirit] will come unto you," "I [the Son] will come unto you," "We [the Father and Son] will come unto you," are interchangeable phrases. The Son comes by or in the Spirit; the Father comes by or in the Son. This is what is called in technical language the doctrine of co-inherence or circuminsession. The divine Three do not act separately or apart as distinct individuals. (Gore, Bampton Lectures, page 145.)

This high and spiritual teaching of the last discourse does not stand alone either in St. John's Gospel or in the Synoptists, though it stands preëminent. (Comp. John i. 1, 18, x. 30, xvii. 5; Matt. xi. 27.)

It prepares us for what we find in the writings of the apostles. In 2 Cor. xiii. 14 (written before any of our Gospels) we have St. Paul in the Apostolic Benediction praying, "The grace of the Lord Jesus Christ, and the love of God, and the communion of the Holy Ghost be with you all." Here is (1) a clear association of Jesus Christ and the Holy Spirit with God as equally objects of worship and sources of blessing; (2) an equally plain recognition of a distinction of personal existence on the part of God, Jesus Christ, and the Holy Spirit.

This passage again stands not alone, though preëminent, among testimonies to the belief of the apostles based on the teaching of the Lord Jesus. (Comp. Eph. iv. 4; Rev. i, 4, 5; 1 John ii, 22, 23.) Other passages will be given under Chapter IV, on the "Incarnation," and in Chapter VII, on the "Holy Ghost."

Such passages demand for their reasonable and harmonious interpretation the Church's doctrine of the Trinity. Without it they would be inconsistent with the recognition of the Unity of the Godhead, which we find taken over from the Old Testament, *e. g*

Mark xii. 32; 1 Corinthians viii. 4; 1 Timothy ii. 5; James ii. 19.[1] The apostles, it must always be remembered, had all been trained in the strictest Monotheism. With this fundamental truth they had to reconcile the teaching of their Master, and their convictions, about Himself and the Spirit He promised to send.

The Essential and the Economic Trinity.— By the doctrine of the Trinity we do not only mean that God has a *three-fold relation to us*, as our Creator, Redeemer, and Sanctifier. This *by itself* would be the error of Sabellius, who taught that the Trinity represented God in three characters; under one aspect He was called the Father, under another aspect the Son, and under a third aspect the Holy Spirit; in other words, that the Father took our nature as the man Christ Jesus; and after dying for our salvation operates on our hearts as the Holy Ghost.[2] We mean that this three-fold relation to us is based upon a *three-fold distinction within Himself*, that God eternally exists in a three-fold mode of being, Father,

---

[1] Hear, O Israel: the LORD our God is one LORD. (Deut. vi. 4, etc.) Hints there were in the Old Testament of a plurality of persons in the Godhead, that we can recognize as we look back from the fuller revelation of the New Testament. (See Gibson, *Thirty-nine Articles*, Vol. I, pp. 93-98; also at the end of A. B. Davidson's article, "God," in *Hastings's Dictionary of the Bible*, Vol. II. p. 205.)

[2] Norris, *Rudiments of Theology*, pp. 32-33, Gibson, *The Three Creeds*, p. 238. This was the reason, that it seemed to favor such a conception, of the Church's rejection of the word πρόσωπα as applied to the Trinity.

Son, and Holy Spirit. The outer relations of the Godhead to the world and to man rest upon the inner relations of the divine life. This conception was forced upon the Church, as we have seen, by the teaching of Christ concerning Himself and concerning the Spirit, if the principle of Monotheism were to be preserved. This conception of a Trinity in Unity once gained, it became fruitful in suggestion of further thoughts about the Godhead. The Son was thought of as eternally mirroring the Father's perfections, and so as the object of the Father's love. This led on to the thought of the Spirit as the bond of love between the Father and the Son.

Whether such thoughts were in the mind of of St. John when he wrote "God is love," is a question of little importance. It was seen that in the light of this thought the words, and the conception of God which they expressed, gained a fuller meaning and justification. God did not *become* love when His creative work was begun. Within His own being He found an adequate object of His contemplation and love. Love is a relation between persons. It is because there are within the Godhead relations which admit of a perfect interchange and reciprocity of affections that God can truly be said to be Love. Thus there is seen to be a richness in the divine life, which is altogether excluded by the thought of God as a solitary unit. In that case His were a barren life, without scope for the exercise of the highest affections. In this light we see that the doctrine of the Trinity has its bearing on practical life. God is

Himself the pattern of social life and of interdependence.[3]

Analogies of the Trinity.— Various analogies of the Trinity may be traced in human life, which may partly (but only, of course, imperfectly) illustrate or shadow forth the divine Threeness in Oneness.

1. Our own created spiritual being (what we speak of as our 'soul') is absolutely one; it cannot be divided, as the body from the soul, or members of the body one from another. But within this real unity there is a distinction of powers or faculties, each having its own function, while the soul acts through each, and all act (or should act) harmoniously; *e. g.* the memory, the understanding, and the will.

We may speak *either* of the memory recalling, the understanding reasoning, and the will deciding, *or* of the person remembering, understanding, choosing. In like manner we speak of God creating, redeeming, sanctifying; *or* we attribute to the Father, as the source of all life, the work of creation, to the Son redemption, to the Holy Spirit sanctification.

As we rise in the scale of being, distinctions become more clear. The distinction in man of faculties rises in God to the higher distinction of persons.

---

[3] Gore, Bampton Lectures, pp. 147, 148; Mason, *Faith of the Gospel*, pp. 53-59; Sanday, Hastings's *Dictionary of the Bible*, Vol. II. pp. 206, 208. For the metaphysical need of plurality in the life of God, and the effect of our conception of the absolute being of God on His relation to us, see R. H. Hutton, *Theological Essays*, "The Incarnation and the Principles of Evidence," p. 231 (second ed.).

2. In created social life we may see a resemblance to the uncreated Trinity. The family (the unit of society) is made up of the man and his wife (his coequal partner) and the child, which is the offspring of them both.

In this illustration the difference must be carefully remembered between, on the one side, the created life which exists *in time*, and, on the other, the uncreated and *eternal* life. In the Godhead there is no earlier and later existence, as in the human family. The divine Son is *always being begotten* by the Father, the Holy Spirit is *always proceeding* from the Father and His coequal and coeternal Son.[4]

The two titles given in Holy Scripture to the Second Person of the Trinity, *the Son* and *the Word* of God, supplement and balance one another. Either would be liable to misinterpretation without the other: (a) By itself the title 'Son' might suggest a later coming into existence; this idea is corrected by the title 'Word' or 'Wisdom.' A word is an uttered thought. Our fragmentary words express the passing thoughts of our minds; the one Word of God discloses His whole mind. God could never have been without His Word. The Son is as essentially present with the Father, in as full and necessary a sense, as the attribute of Wisdom is ever with Him. (b) On the other hand, the title 'Son' gives an em-

---

[4] ἀεὶ γεννᾶται, Origen, *Hom. in Jerem.* ix. 4. Comp. *De Principiis*, I. 5: "His generation is as eternal and everlasting as the brilliancy which is produced from the sun," and Athanasius: "Begotten, not by the will of the Father, but by the necessity of the Father's nature."—(*Orat. contr. Arian.* iii. 62.)

phasis to the idea of personal existence which is lacking in the title 'Word.' The use of both titles reminds us that all our language must be inadequate to express divine mysteries. Human terms can only be used of God by way of accommodation to our finite intelligence.[5]

The term 'Person' used of the Trinity.— The term 'Person' in English suggests a greater distinction than is intended when we speak of the Trinity, as the Latin *persona* comes short of the truth.[6] By 'persons'

---

[5] All attempts to explain the nature and relations of the Deity must largely depend on metaphor, and no one metaphor can exhaust these relations. Each metaphor can only describe one aspect of the nature or being of the Deity, and the inferences which can be drawn from it have their limits when they conflict with the inferences which can be truly drawn from other metaphors describing other aspects.— (Bethune-Baker, *Introduction to the History of Christian Doctrine*, p. 160.)

[6] " There is but one person in God, in the sense in which we now use the word; but in the one divine personality there are three different modes of subsistence, and to these the Latin fathers applied the term *persona*, while the Greeks used *hypostasis*." Steenstra, *The Being of God*, p. 189. *Hypostasis* in popular Greek signified something solid and firm. It was adopted in the language of philosophy to signify the reality underlying an appearance or a mental conception. This was not far removed from Being or Substance, and at times it was understood as an equivalent to οὐσία. But in Christian theology it was strictly used to express the severalty of the Father, the Son, and the Holy Spirit. There was danger in this term so used; danger of its being taken to mean too separate an existence, as the Latin word *persona* might easily imply too little separation. For the history of the use of the terms οὐσία and ὑπόστασις, see Gibson, *Articles*, I. pp. 107-111.

as applied to the Trinity we do not mean three separate individual beings (which is the sense in which we use the word of our fellow men). These might be of a different character, and so forth, whereas in the Godhead there is but one will, one love, one holiness. The Son is of one substance (or essence) with the Father; that is, not only of one eternal, infinite and uncreated being; of one omnipresence, omnipotence and omniscience, but likewise of one moral being, of one love, truth, justice and holiness.

This excludes any parcelling out of the divine attributes (such as has often prevailed in popular theology), so that the Father was thought of as all justice and holiness, while mercy and love were embodied in the Son. It was this dualistic conception of God (clean contrary to the Scriptural representation) which led by a perfectly natural reaction to the Unitarianism of Channing.[7] The Son is the "express image," the exact representation of the Father; the Word made flesh acts out in our nature and amid our circumstances God's character, so that Christ could say, "he that hath seen me hath seen the Father." (Heb. i. 3, John xiv. 9.)

The doctrine of the Monarchia and of Subordination.— The unity of the Godhead is further emphasized by what is called the doctrine of the Monarchia, which guards the force of the term Father applied to

---

[7] Tritheism is belief in three separate Principles, or the division of the divine substance among three several Beings. Unitarianism is the denial of the existence of personal relations in the divine substance.

the first person of the Trinity, regarding Him as the fount of deity in the eternal life of the Trinity, from whom Son and Holy Spirit derive their divine being. This is in accordance with Christ's own words, "As the Father hath life in himself, even so gave he to the Son to have life in himself." (John v. 26; comp. vi. 57, and xvi. 13-15.) With the recognition of this truth follows the Subordination of the Son, whose being is eternally derived, to the Father, whose being is underived, and of the Holy Spirit to the Father and the Son, as deriving His being from both. The term subordination implies not inferiority, but derivation.[8]

This distinction of persons in oneness of being, this subordination in equality, this derivation in coeternal life, is summarily expressed by Hooker:

"'The Lord our God is but one God.' In which indivisible unity notwithstanding we adore the Father as being altogether of himself, we glorify that consubstantial Word which is the Son, we bless and magnify that co-essential Spirit eternally proceeding from both which is the Holy Ghost. Seeing therefore the Father is of none, the Son is of the Father, and the Spirit is of both, they are by these their several properties really distinguishable each from other. For the substance of God with this property *to be of none* doth make the Person of the Father; the very selfsame substance in number with this property *to be of the Father* maketh the Person of the Son; the same substance having added unto it the property of *pro-*

---

[8] Liddon, Bampton Lectures, pp. 202, 310. *Westcott, St. John's Gospel*, detached note on xiv. 28.

ceeding from the other two maketh the Person of the Holy Ghost. So that in every Person there is implied both the substance of God, which is one, and also that property which causeth the same person really and truly to differ from the other two. Every person hath his own subsistence which no other besides hath, although there be others besides that are of the same substance."—(Eccl. Pol. V. li.)

It is the same Scriptural truth that is stated rather than explained, and in a form easy to commit to memory, in the Athanasian Hymn, *Quicunque vult*.

The Catholic Faith is this: That we worship one God in Trinity, and Trinity in Unity;

Neither confounding the Persons: nor dividing the Substance.

For there is one Person of the Father, another of the Son: and another of the Holy Ghost.

But the Godhead of the Father, of the Son, and of the Holy Ghost, is all one: the Glory equal, the Majesty co-eternal.

Such as the Father is, such is the Son: and such is the Holy Ghost.

The Father uncreate, the Son uncreate: and the Holy Ghost uncreate.

The Father incomprehensible, the Son incomprehensible: and the Holy Ghost incomprehensible.

The Father eternal, the Son eternal: and the Holy Ghost eternal.

And yet they are not three eternals: but one eternal.

As also there are not three incomprehensibles, nor

three uncreated: but one uncreated, and one incomprehensible.

So likewise the Father is Almighty, the Son Almighty: and the Holy Ghost Almighty.

And yet they are not three Almighties: but one Almighty.

So the Father is God, the Son is God: and the Holy Ghost is God.

And yet they are not three Gods: but one God.

So likewise the Father is Lord, the Son Lord: and the Holy Ghost Lord.

And yet not three Lords: but one Lord.

For like as we are compelled by the Christian verity: to acknowledge every Person by himself to be God and Lord;

So are we forbidden by the Catholic Religion: to say, There be three Gods, or three Lords.

The Father is made of none: neither created, nor begotten.

The Son is of the Father alone: not made, nor created, but begotten.

The Holy Ghost is of the Father and of the Son: neither made, nor created, nor begotten, but proceeding.

So there is one Father, not three Fathers; one Son, not three Sons: one Holy Ghost, not three Holy Ghosts.

And in this Trinity none is afore, or after other: none is greater, or less than another;

But the whole three Persons are co-eternal together: and co-equal.

So that in all things, as is aforesaid: the Unity in Trinity, and the Trinity in Unity is to be worshipped.

BIBLIOGRAPHY

J. R. Illingworth, " The Doctrine of the Trinity."

W. N. Clark, " Outlines of Christian Theology." Part I. § iv.

R. C. Moberly, " Atonement and Personality," Chap. VIII.

D. Waterland, " The Importance of the Doctrine of the Trinity."

P. H. Streenstra, " The Being of God as Unity and Trinity."

E. C. S. Gibson, " The Thirty-nine Articles," Article I.

A. J. Mason, " The Faith of the Gospel," Chapter II.

Leighton Pullan, " Lectures on Religion," Chapter IV.

J. P. Norris, " Rudiments of Theology," Pt. I, Chapters II and IV.

Darwell Stone, " Outlines of Christian Dogma," Chapter III.

T. A. Lacey, " The Elements of Christian Doctrine," Chapter I, sect. ii.

T. Christlieb, " Modern Doubt and Christian Belief," Lect IV.

2, *Trinitarian Conception of the Divine Nature.*

S. Augustine, *De Trinitate.*

H. Lotze, " Microcosmus," Vol. II. p. 486 ff. 4th edition.

I. A. Dorner, " A System of Christian Doctrine," Vol. II. Pt. 1. (Clark's Theological Library.)

Dawson Walker, " One God or Three ?" (English Church Manuals.)

The Editor would refer those interested in the trinitarian conceptions which are found in other religions to W. Williamson " The Great Law," Book I, Chapter IX.

IV.

THE INCARNATION

The Incarnation the climax of God's self-manifestation.— By the Incarnation is meant the union of human nature with divine nature in the one person of God the Son. "The Word was made flesh" (John i. 14). This is the climax of God's self-manifestation. (1) He had made Himself known through Nature, which bears the impress of its Maker's power and wisdom (Rom. i. 20; Ps. xix. 1; Acts xiv. 17). (2) In History and by His Providence He had more clearly revealed His moral character, guiding events and bringing about the triumph of truth and justice. (3) In the Conscience of all men the Word of God spoke, giving a knowledge of right and wrong, however confused the lines may often have become (Rom. ii. 5; John i. 9). (4) Through the Prophets, men whom He raised up to receive and transmit His message, He made known more of His mind and will, and that in increasing measure (Heb. i. 1). These were not confined to the Jewish people, though Israel was preëminently the sacred school for all the world of religious instruction. (Ath. *de Inc.* xii.) In the fulness of time (Gal. iv. 4), the stage of God's final revelation of Himself in this world, the Word of God Himself became flesh, took human nature, and therein acted out God's true character, translated the divine perfections into language that we can understand, the language of human conduct; and at the same time shewed what man's life should be. "What Jesus was, God is. What Jesus was, man should be, and by His help may more and more become."

Four great doctrinal decisions.— The various points of doctrine in the Incarnation may conveniently be considered under the four great decisions at which Christian thought, represented and expressed by great representative Councils of the Church, arrived through the controversies of the fourth and fifth centuries. These can hardly be better expressed than in Hooker's words: "There are but four things which concur to make complete the whole state of our Lord Jesus Christ: his Deity, his manhood, the conjunction of both, and the distinction of the one from the other being joined in one. Four principal heresies there are which have in those things withstood the truth: Arians by bending themselves against the Deity of Christ; Apollinarians by maiming and misinterpreting that which belongeth to his human nature; Nestorians by rending Christ asunder, and dividing him into two persons; the followers of Eutyches by confounding in his person those natures which they should distinguish. Against these there have been four most famous ancient general councils: the council of Nice [A. D. 325] to define against Arians, against Apollinarians the council of Constantinople [A. D. 381], the council of Ephesus [A. D. 431] against Nestorians, against Eutychians the Chalcedon coun_ cil [A. D. 451]. In four words, ἀληθῶς, τελέως, ἀδιαιρέτως, ἀσυγχύτως — *truly, perfectly, indivisibly, distinctly;* the first applied to his being God, and the second to his being Man, the third to his being of both One, and the fourth to his still continuing in that one Both: we may fully by way of abridgment comprise whatsoever antiquity hath at large handled either in declaration of Christian belief, or in refutation of the foresaid heresies. Within the compass of which four heads, I may truly affirm, that all heresies which touch but the person of Jesus Christ, whether they have risen in these later days, or in any age heretofore, may be with great facility brought to confine themselves." (Eccl. Pol. V. liv. 10.)

In somewhat simpler language the "four definitions which the Church universal has made binding" may be thus summarized:

(1) "That Christ is of one substance with the Father;

(2) that He was completely human;

(3) that His humanity had no independent centre of personality in itself;

(4) but that in the unity of the one divine person both Godhead and manhood remain, two natures in one person."— (Gore, *The New Theology and the Old Religion*, p. 191.)

I. *Christ truly God.*— Our Lord's earliest disciples first became convinced that *Jesus* of Nazareth, their Master, was *the Christ*, the long-expected Messenger and Representative of God, for whom Israel was looking, whose coming and work had been foretold under divers titles and figures by the prophets of old. Promises that primarily had a wider scope, referring to the chosen nation, as the seed of Abraham (Gen. xxii. 18) or to the royal line of David (2 Sam. vii. 12-16; Ps. lxxxix. 19-37), or to the prophetic order (Deut. xviii. 15), were seen in the light of later prophecies, especially those concerning the Servant of the Lord (Isa. xl-liii; Matt. xii. 18), to be concentrated on a *personal* representative of the nation, in whom the Lord would manifest Himself, to judge, redeem, and govern His people.[1] The Messiah or the Christ (in English the Anointed One) was the title given to the expected Messenger. While He was to be a Prophet to make God's will fully known, and a Priest to reconcile the people to God, His function was chiefly that of a King to rule over the people in God's name (Pss. ii, lxxii; Isa. ix, xi, xxxii; Dan. ii. 44, vii. 27).[2]

---

[1] "The deepest and most permanent element pervading the varied imagery of the prophets is the thought of the advent of Jehovah Himself to judge, redeem, and govern His people, and to sanctify them by the bestowal of His Spirit. (Ezek. xxxvi. 25-27, xxxvii. 27.) The Redeemer who should come to Zion would be Himself divine." (Comp. Isa. lix. 16-20; Amos iv. 12; Isa. ii. xxxii.)—(Ottley on " The Incarnation " in Hastings's *Dictionary of the Bible*, II. p. 459.)

[2] "He will be the ideal king, whose mind and action shall be in entire accord with the will of God, who will be God's true representative upon earth, in whose day and through whom God will make good all His promises, and who will lead all men to honor the God of Israel, and to respect Israel as God's people." (V. H. Stanton, art. "Messiah," in Hasting's *Dictionary of the Bible*, II. p. 353.)

While for the most part the Jews of our Lord's time had an earthly conception of the Messiah's work and reign, trusting that he would throw off the yoke of the Roman conqueror and restore Israel again to a high place among the nations, they generally looked for a supernatural Messiah, of more than human dignity (John vii. 27). He was commonly thought of as in some way preëxisting.[3]

Accordingly, convinced by His words and works that their Master was "the Coming One," the disciples during His earthly ministry acknowledged Jesus as the Son of God in some special and unique sense (Matt. xvi. 16, xiv. 33).

Later, after reflexion and with the aid of the Holy Spirit, they came to see that the words they used had a deeper and higher meaning than they had realized or intended when they used them. They came to believe that Jesus was not merely a great Prophet and Messenger — the expected Messiah, but that He was the Son of God become man, not a man on whom Divine influence had come in altogether unique fashion, but in His inmost being, His real person, God. This conviction these disciples gathered:

(a) from their Master's *claims* which were altogether inconsistent with moral excellence in any created being: *e. g.* to be the universal and final judge (Matt. xxv. 31); to give rest and satisfy the spiritual needs

---

[3] There was a thought of the Messiah as preëxisting in some extra-territorial region, partly based on Dan. vii. This could be harmonized with the thought of a descendant of David having been first caught up from the earth and preserved for a glorious manifestation. (*Ibid.* p. 355.)

of all (Matt. xi. 28-30); requiring absolute obedience and devotion (Mark viii. 38); associating Himself with God (Matt. xi. 28-30, xxviii. 19; John x. 29, 30); never admitting any fault (John viii. 46); attributing virtue to His death (Mark xiv. 24), reviewing God's law (Matt. v. 21, 22, etc.).

(b) from seeing what the prophecies really involved (*e. g.* Isa. xl. 3; Zech. xiii. 7; Ps. cx. 1; Isa. ix), and how the prophecies were "fulfilled" in Him;

(c) from His life (John i. 14, 1 John i. 1-3);

(d) from His resurrection (Rom. i. 4; John xx. 28).

This belief the apostles manifested by rendering to Him divine worship and utter self devotion (Phil. i. 1); by associating Him with the Father, as the Object of doxologies (Rev. i. 5, 6, v. 13); as the Source of blessings (2 Cor. i. 2 and xiii. 14).

The problem which early Christians had to face, which the Church had later to think out, was, how to harmonize this recognition of Christ's divinity with the fundamental truth (in which the apostles as Jews had all been grounded) of Monotheism, *i. e.* that there is but One Supreme Being.

The answer of the Church (based on our Lord's own teaching, recorded in the New Testament Scriptures), was the doctrine of the Trinity, that within the absolute and indivisible Oneness of the Divine Being there is a three-fold mode of life. (See Chapter III. on the Trinity, p. 51). From all eternity the Father had His co-equal Son, essentially one with Him as His Wisdom or Word. It was by the agency of this Word, the utterance of God's mind, that all things in the beginning were created. The Son was Himself not created, as something external to the Divine Being, but begotten; God's own and only Son by nature, sharing all His Father's attributes; God the Son of God (John i. 18), Light streaming forth from Light, of one substance or essence with the Father.

This was the final answer of the Nicene fathers to the question forced upon the Church by various speculations, and at last by the heresy of Arius, who, while giving all manner of lofty titles to our Lord, flatly denied that the divine Son was coeternal with the Father, making Him the highest of all created beings, but really external to the divine essence.

(1) Thus are excluded not only mere humanitarian conceptions of our Lord, but likewise any idea of Him as a secondary deity. It was against any such notion as this that Athanasius persistently argued in opposition to the semi-Arians, as fatal to Christianity, as a relapse, however unintentional, into Pagan polytheism.

(2) This formal declaration of belief in our Lord's Godhead, contained in the Nicene Creed, its framers and upholders always contended was no new article of faith; it was only the explicit statement of what the Church had always believed, a definition called forth and rendered necessary by the denial or explaining away of the meaning of earlier and simpler professions of belief. "Thus we have received," "so we believe," was the testimony of the representatives of all parts of Christendom.

(3) In all the explanations thus given to safeguard the truth, orthodox theologians have been careful to insist on the inadequacy of human language to express divine relations. It was the rationalistic argument of Arius that since an earthly father was prior to his son, therefore the Divine Son must be later in origin than His Father. The faulty logic of this argument was easily shown when it was pointed out that sequence of *time* does not belong to God and His life; but that it really belongs to the *essence* of the filial relation to share the father's nature (whatever that may be).

But, while refuting false by true logical reasoning, Athanasius and his followers always insisted that the human mind is no true measure for the Divine Being. We must be content with an intelligent grasp of what is revealed, without expecting that we can comprehend all that we apprehend.

II. *Christ completely Man.*— The Son of God, who is of one substance with the Father, became man, taking human nature in its completeness. There were ancient heretics (the Docetics) who regarded the human body of Christ as a mere phantom. This error is far removed from our thought. The reality of the body in which Christ was born; which received nourishment and grew, which suffered hunger, weariness and pain, which was slain and buried, is to us unquestionable.

A more subtle error was that of Apollinaris, who supposed that the Eternal Logos took the place in Christ of the rational human soul (the νοῦς as distinct from the ψυχή). This position was adopted in a reaction from Arianism, in the endeavor to put as great a difference as possible between our Lord and any created being. The Word of God was thought of as becoming directly the controlling power and principle of the physical elements of Christ's nature.

Any such idea is expressly excluded by the witness of the New Testament Scriptures, which tell not only —

of Christ's growth in *bodily* stature, but also of His advance in *intellectual* wisdom (Luke i. 52);
of His *affections*; of love (John xi. 5, Mark x. 21), and anger (Mark iii. 5), of joy (Luke xi. 21), and grief (John xi. 35, Luke xix. 41, Mark xiv. 34), of hope (Heb. xii. 2), and fear (Heb. v. 7);
of His human *will*, which He surrendered to His Father's will (Luke xxii. 42).

Moreover the Scriptures point to a *moral* advance, not from bad to good, but from the perfection of flawlessness to the perfection of ripened maturity, as He advanced in favor with God as well as with man, (Luke ii. 52), as He learned obedience by the things which He suffered (Heb. v. 8), and was made perfect through sufferings (Heb. ii. 10).

With these testimonies to the completeness of Christ's manhood should be considered the many instances of His praying, lifting up, that is, His human heart to God in communion with His Father, and calling forth His power, showing that His human nature was subject to the law not only of growth but of dependence which belongs to all created and finite beings.[4] In the power of the anointing Spirit He performed His ministry (Luke iv. 1, 18, v. 16, 17; Acts x. 38).

It is clear from these passages that the word "flesh" in John i. 14 is not used in an exclusive sense, as referring only to the body. It rather stands for human nature on the side of its frailty. (Comp. John iii. 6; Matt. xvi. 17, xxiv. 22.) The Son of God took all the elements of our nature, even the lowest.

It was in accordance with this teaching of Scripture that the Church emphasized in the Creed Christ's birth of a human mother, showing Him to be really one with us, as He is really one with God.

Our Proper Preface for the Christmas festival bears witness to the same truth:

"Thou didst give Jesus Christ, thine only Son, to be born as at this time for us; who, by the operation of the Holy Ghost, was made very man, of the substance of the Virgin Mary his mother; and that without spot of sin, to make us clean from all sin."

Thus are guarded the reality of Christ's *sympathy*, the truth of His *example*, the rescue and *restoration of our whole nature*. All these would be lost, if Christ had no human will, with power of choice and de-

---

[4] See *The Prayers of Jesus Christ*, by C. J. Vaughan. The instances of our Lord's own prayers are all given in an Appendix to *The Christian Doctrine of Prayer* (Bohlen Lectures), by the author.

termination, on which depends the real character of human conduct.

"He was made *man*." Whatever is necessary to human nature, all that makes man man, all the constituents of a normal human experience, He took upon Himself.

Sin does not belong to human nature, however universal an accompaniment it may be in our experience. Like physical disease, sin is an abnormal accident, a disorder to be rectified. When the Son of God took our nature, by the Spirit's quickening power, of a Virgin mother, He took it free from disorder. Body, mind, heart, and soul were in perfect correspondence with God's design for man's nature. It was in the likeness of 'sinful flesh,' subject to temptation, bearing the external penalty of man's transgression, encompassed with evil in the world around; only by struggle could its purity be preserved, its perfect development be secured.[4] By this struggle a *moral* victory was gained over sin and

---

[4] Roman. viii. 3. "St. Paul declares that the Father sent His own Son to redeem us in 'the likeness of the flesh of sin.' The word 'likeness' [$\dot{o}\mu o \iota \omega \mu a$] is the same as that used in the similar passage (Phil. ii. 7), where we are told that the eternal Son in love for us 'emptied Himself' so far as to take the 'form' [$\mu o \rho \phi \dot{\eta}$], or essential characteristics, of our servile human nature; nor only its essential characteristics, but also the outward conditions or 'likeness' of common men as they are. The point is that Christ, who Himself as man 'knew no sin' [2 Cor. v. 21], appeared amongst us under all the circumstances of sin, and with no outward or apparent difference between us and Him — 'in all points like as we are' with the single exception of sin in the will or in the nature."— (Gore on Ep. to the Romans, Vol. I, pp. 278, 279.)

Satan. Man, who had been defeated, reversed the defeat in the person of Christ, his human powers being aided by the Spirit of God. (Gen. iii. 15.)

Thus was given a fresh start to human nature. Christ became a Second Adam, a fount of renewed humanity, of which we are made partakers by the Spirit of God and through the sacraments Christ has ordained for this purpose. In Him all are to be made alive.

III. *Christ one indivisible Person.*— It is especially to the union of the two natures, human and divine, in the one person of Christ, that Hooker's saying is applied: While the mystery, as taught in Holy Scripture, is more true than plain, many human speculations concerning it are more plain than true. (Eccl. Pol. V. lii. 1.) On the one hand, there is the error of Nestorianism (whether Nestorius was personally involved in it or not),[5] which, insisting on the completeness of the human nature assumed by the Son of God, attributed to it a distinct human personality, or independent centre of action. Thus an association of persons (the Son of Mary with the Son of God) was substituted for a union of natures in the one eternal person of the Son or Word of God, who, without ceasing to be all that He ever was, became man, taking to Himself a complete human nature, subject to all the laws that govern human nature. Of the manner or extent in which the human nature was affected by the divine with which it was conjoined in the person of Christ, we cannot tell. (Hooker,

---

[5] See J. F. Bethune-Baker, "Nestorius and Nestorianism."

Eccl. Pol. V. liv. 7, 8.) He lived His human life as man, subject to the limitations of the manhood which He had assumed. It would appear from the Gospels that it was only on exceptional occasions and for great purposes connected with His mission that He permitted the almighty power or the infinite wisdom of His Godhead to penetrate the physical and intellectual faculties of His human nature.

It ought to be kept in mind (but often is not) that the Eternal Word was not confined in His presence or operations to the human form in which He manifested Himself on earth. He was still and ever in the bosom of the Father —

> *Verbum supernum prodiens*
> *Nec Patris linquens dexteram,—*

still and ever upholding all things, and lightening every man (John i. 9; Heb. i. 3; Col. i. 16, 17). To focus the sun's rays on a particular spot is not to give an exclusive possession of them to that spot.[6]

It is all important for a right understanding of the Incarnation that our thought should always begin with the divine person who became man. Defective theories for the most part are based on the thought of a human person upon whom, in altogether unique measure, divine influence came, in like manner as

---

[6] "Whatever of self-limitation was necessary, He always remained in possession of His powers, recognizing a law of restraint where restraint was necessary." "The measure of the self-restraint is the capacity of the perfect manhood to receive, assimilate, and coöperate with divine power." (F. Weston, *The One Christ*, pp. 136, 139.)

upon the prophets. The "I" in Christ, the centre of His being, is divine. (See Appendix D.)

Against any conception of an alliance between a holy man, Jesus, and the Word of God, the Council of Ephesus (A. D. 431) approved the title θεοτόκος (Mother of God, or rather God-bearer) applied to the blessed Virgin Mary; not, of course, meaning thereby that Mary was, in any sense, the mother of Christ's divine nature, but that He who was born of her in His human nature, was God the Son.[7]

In connection with this title (given not for the honour of Mary but to safeguard the dignity of her Son), should be remembered the theological phrase, the *Communicatio idiomatum*, or "interchange of properties." This means that, recognizing the singleness of the personality of Christ, and at the same time the indissoluble union of the humanity with this one Divine Person, we are at liberty to use expressions properly belonging to one nature only, of the Person, who as Incarnate possesses both.—(Strong, *Manual of Theology*, p. 116.)

---

[7] In the Greek word θεοτόκος the component θεός is logically a *predicate*, and as such is absolutely justified and covered by the Catholic doctrine. On the other hand, in the English phrase *Mother of God*, 'God' is practically a subject rather than a predicate, and therefore includes logically the person of the Father. θεοτόκος, *Deipara*, God-bearer, are not strictly equivalent to μητὴρ θεοῦ, *Mater Dei*, Mother of God. —(Bethune-Baker, *Early History of Christian Doctrine*, pp. 262, 263.)

Scriptural Predicates:

What is human of God—	*What is divine of Man—*
e. g. The Word was made flesh (John i. 14).	*e. g.* The Son of man who is in heaven (John iii. 13).
God purchased the Church with his own blood (Acts xx. 28).	
The princes of this world crucified the Lord of glory (1 Cor. ii. 8).	
That which was from the beginning, which we have seen and our hands handled, of the Word of Life (1 John i. 1).	

i. e. not of the Godhead, but	*i. e. not of the Manhood, but*
of Christ's one Person	
in His manhood	*in His Godhead.*[8]

"The solution of the Nestorian difficulties, so far as it was a solution, was reached in the teaching that it was not the person of *a* man that was assumed by the Logos, but *man; i. e.*, human nature, human characteristics and attributes, which could be taken up by the divine Person, the Logos, and entered upon and made His own."

"The Person who enters upon the conditions of human life, and accepts the limitation of His divine

---

[8] W. Bright, *S. Leo on the Incarnation*, p. 130 (2d ed).

life which is involved by those conditions, is divine; but all the human experiences are his, and in that sense he is human too."—(Bethune-Baker, *Early History of Christian Doctrine*, p. 294.)

IV. *The divine and human natures unconfused.*—The opposite error to Nestorianism, and a reaction therefrom, is Eutychianism, which, contending against a dual personality in Christ, confounded the divine and human natures, regarding the manhood as practically absorbed in the Godhead. This would really result in a composite nature, half human, half divine, and Christ would be neither man nor God. Any such confusion of natures and their properties the Church condemns, maintaining a true distinction between the divine and the human, and the integrity of each in its own sphere.

Ubiquitarianism.— The form in which this error perhaps most commonly meets us is a vague idea of Christ's human nature as being now ubiquitous. This notion arises in part from a failure to distinguish between the *person* of Christ, the incarnate Son of God, and the human *nature*, which He assumed and ever wears. As the Son of God *He* is present everywhere, and since He became man we have the assurance of His *sympathy* gained by human experience, and of the *fellowship* with us that comes from sharing our nature. He *who is the Son of Man* is present everywhere. But this is quite different from supposing that His *human nature*, even now that it is exalted to the right hand of God, is exempted from all the limitations that belong to it as something created and finite. Christ can manifest Himself in His human nature to whom and as He will; the Spirit takes of the things of Christ and imparts them to us, not only truth to our intelligence, but the virtue also of His glorified humanity through the Sacraments. But His human nature remains subject to limitation.

"Supernatural endowments are an advancement, they are no extinguishment of that nature whereto they are given."—(Hooker, *Eccl. Pol.* V. lv. 6.)

A balanced statement of the Church's doctrine on the Incarnation thought out through the controversies of the fourth and fifth centuries, is given in the second part of the *Quicunque vult:*

The right Faith is, that we believe and confess: that our Lord Jesus Christ, the Son of God, is God and Man;

God, of the Substance of the Father, begotten before the worlds: and Man, of the Substance of his Mother, born in the world;

Perfect God, and perfect Man: of a reasonable soul and human flesh subsisting;

Equal to the Father, as touching his Godhead: and inferior to the Father, as touching his Manhood.

Who although he be God and Man: yet he is not two, but one Christ;

One; not by conversion of the Godhead into flesh: but by taking of the Manhood into God;

One altogether; not by confusion of Substance: but by unity of Person.

For as the reasonable soul and flesh is one man: so God and Man is one Christ;

Who suffered for our salvation: descended into hell, rose again the third day from the dead.

He ascended into heaven, he sitteth on the right hand of the Father, God Almighty: from whence he shall come to judge the quick and the dead.

With this may be compared the teaching on these points of the second of the Articles of Religion:

Of the Word or Son of God, which was made very Man.— The Son, which is the Word of the Father, begotten from everlasting of the Father, the very and eternal God, and of one substance with the Father, took Man's nature in the womb of the blessed Virgin, of her substance: so that two whole and perfect Natures, that is to say, the Godhead and Manhood, were joined together in one Person, never to be divided, whereof is one Christ, very God, and very Man.

BIBLIOGRAPHY

G. Bull, " Defence of the Nicene Creed."

R. Hooker, " Ecclesiastical Polity," book V. cc. l-lvii.

H. P. Liddon, " The Divinity of our Lord and Saviour Jesus Christ" (Bampton Lectures, 1866).

C. Gore, " The Incarnation of the Son of God" (Bampton Lectures, 1891).

C. Gore, " Dissertations on subjects connected with the Incarnation."

I. A. Dorner, " Doctrine of the Person of Christ."

R. L. Ottley, " The Doctrine of the Incarnation."

R. I. Wilberforce " The Doctrine of the Incarnation."

H. C. Powell, " The Principle of the Incarnation."

A. J. Mason, " The Conditions of our Lord's Life on earth" (Paddock Lectures, 1896).

E. H. Gifford, " The Incarnation" (a study of Phil. ii. 5-11).

H. V. S. Eck, " The Incarnation" (Oxford Library of Practical Theology).

V. H. Stanton, " The Jewish and the Christian Messiah."

W. P. DuBose, " The Gospel in the Gospels."

W. P. DuBose, "The Ecumenical Councils."

W. Bright, " The Age of the Fathers."

W. Bright, " S. Leo on the Incarnation," with notes.

J. F. Bethune-Baker, " Introduction to the early history of Christian Doctrine."

F. Weston, " The One Christ."

C. L. Slattery, " The Master of the World."

F. Bruce. " The Humiliation of Christ."

C. A. Briggs, " The Virgin Birth of our Lord."

James Orr, " The Virgin Birth of Christ."

J. Armitage Robinson, " Some Thoughts on the Incarnation."

E. Griffith-Jones, " Ascent Through Christ," Bk. II., cc. i, ii.

V.

THE ATONEMENT

The Fall of man.—"For us men and for our salvation," that is, for our rescue and restoration, the Eternal Son of God took our nature and lived our life. Whether the Incarnation would have taken place apart from the need of man's rescue is a question that has been debated by theologians.[1] It need not here claim our attention. As a matter of fact, human nature had fallen into disorder; man was not living in correspondence with God's design for him. He had been deceived by appearances, and had sought happiness in passing pleasure and in the indulgence of the lower desires of his nature at the expense of the higher. Appetites and whims had carried captive what should have been the ruling powers of reason and conscience. Thus he had fallen under the bondage of the Evil One. From this condition he needed rescue and restoration. To procure and bestow this the Son of God, by whom as the Father's agent all things at the first were made, entered this world in human form, that He might win man back to his true allegiance, and therein to his true freedom, dignity and welfare.

The fall of man is represented to us in Genesis iii.

---

[1] For the Scotist and Thomist theories, see D. Stone, *Outlines of Christian Dogma*, p. 55, and Westcott's *Epistles of St. John*, pp. 273-275.

under a figurative description.[2] What is clear is this, that man, however imperfectly developed, was in the favor of God. By an act of disobedience he forfeited that favor; instead of rising higher by the right exercise of his power of choice in accordance with God's will, he fell from his true dignity, and his progress was retarded. "Sin is the disobedience of intelligent beings whom God has created, and whom He has endowed with a free will, which they can use or misuse."[3] God's commandments are not arbitrary, however little we at the time may realize their purpose. They mark out the path of our peace and well being. Man's disobedience to God is consequently a contravention of the laws of his own being. Sin is lawlessness ($\dot{a}\nu o\mu ia$), and necessarily involves ruin individual and social (1 John iii. 4). By this violation of the law of his being, disorder is introduced, and spiritual death ensues, the forfeiture of God's hallowing presence, from which man has withdrawn. Of this inner spiritual death, the death of the body is an outward figure and expression.[4]

Transmission of disordered nature.— The transmission of a disordered spiritual nature, however difficult the problems which it suggests, is in line with what science and observation teach us about

---

[2] An excellent vindication of "the story-like form in which the Hebrew prophet couched his sublime teaching" is given in Lecture V. of Curteis's Boyle Lectures on *Scientific Obstacles to Christian Belief*.

[3] J. B. Lightfoot, *St. Paul's Epistle to the Colossians*, p. 185.

[4] Rom. v. 12-15. See Note D in Vol. II. of Gore's *Exposition of the Epistle to the Romans*.

heredity, and about the very close and intimate connexion between the material and the spiritual elements of man's being. We must guard against an exaggeration and caricature of the doctrine of original sin. The sin of our parents or of our first parents is not *imputed* to us, nor are we *punished* for their transgressions, however we may be involved in the consequences thereof. The sin or sinful condition in which we are born is to be regarded chiefly as the result of the loss of a supernatural gift of grace, by which God intended that our nature should be raised to its true dignity of conscious dependence on God and fellowship with Him. Without this grace as a guiding and controlling principle our nature loses its harmony and right direction. Observation and experience shew us in human nature (as we know it) a bias towards evil, and a consciousness of disorder in the universal sense of shame.

The Atonement variously represented.— The Atonement is the making at one of God and man. This is represented in the New Testament Scriptures in many aspects and under various figures. These mark out lines of thought by which we are encouraged to seek an intelligent grasp of the mystery, which doubtless involves much that is beyond our fathoming:

1. By the *manifestation of God's love* in Christ, His incarnate Son, man is won back from erroneous conceptions of God as a stern and hard taskmaster, or a distant ruler indifferent to the fate of His creatures.

"God commendeth his own love toward us, in that, while we were yet sinners, Christ died for us"

(Rom. v. 8). God's love, we must always remember, as we are plainly taught in Holy Scripture, was the moving cause, not the result, of what Christ did. "God so loved the world, that he gave his only begotten Son, that whosoever believeth in him should not perish, but have eternal life" (John iii. 16).

2. By the splendid *example of a perfect human life* which Christ gave, man is attracted and weaned from false conceptions of life and happiness. By His example, as by His teaching, Christ corrects our ordinary estimate of values. Putting aside wealth, pleasure and the world's honors, He showed that man's life consists not in what he has, but in what he is; that self-sacrifice for others brings truer happiness than self-assertion or self-seeking; that virtue is more to be prized than fame, and God's approval and love than the world's applause. Lifted up on the cross of shame and suffering Christ draws all to Himself, by the moral beauty of His example, as well as by the assurance of His sympathy.

3. By *wrestling with temptation Christ rescues man* from bondage to evil. Neither the English word 'redeem,' nor the Hebrew and Greek words for which it is used as a translation, necessarily convey any idea of a price paid. The word is often simply equivalent to the effecting of deliverance or emancipation. In this sense it is frequently used with reference to the deliverance of Israel from bondage in Egypt or from captivity in Babylon; *e. g.* "Say unto the children of Israel, I am the LORD, and I will bring you out from under the burdens of the Egyptians, and I will rid you out of their bondage, and I

will redeem you with an outstretched arm, and with great judgments" (Ex. vi. 6).

"Thou in thy loving kindness hast led the people that thou hast redeemed: Thou hast guided them in thy strength to thy holy habitation" (Ex. xv. 13).

"Thus saith the LORD that created thee, O Jacob, and he that formed thee, O Israel: Fear not, for I have redeemed thee; I have called thee by thy name, thou art mine" (Isa. xliii. 1).

"The LORD hath redeemed Jacob, and will glorify himself in Israel" (Isa. xliv. 23).

So, in a more general way, of the Messiah it is sung, He shall redeem or deliver His people from oppression and violence: precious shall their blood be in his sight. (Ps. lxxii. 14.)

There is no idea of payment here; rather the thought is of the display of might; the Redeemer is the Avenger.

In this sense Christ redeems or delivers man from the power of sin and Satan. "He shall save His people from their sins" (Matt. i. 21). "Ye were redeemed, not with corruptible things, with silver or gold, from your vain manner of life handed down from your fathers; but with precious blood, as of a lamb without blemish and without spot, *even the blood* of Christ" (1 Pet. i. 18).

"He gave himself for us, that he might redeem us from all iniquity, and purify unto himself a people for his own possession, zealous of good works." (Tit. ii. 14; comp. Gal. i. 3, 4.)

This moral emancipation could not be effected by the mere display of force. It could only be accomplished by moral exertion, by the putting forth of spiritual power, by wrestling with temptation and resisting the Evil One. This involves pain and struggle. So does Jesus Christ deliver us at the cost of His blood, of His life spent and laid down in battling against our spiritual foes. (1 Pet. i. 18; Eph. i. 7.)

This is the figure under which the restoration of man is first promised in Holy Scripture. The seed of the woman, at the expense of his own heel being bruised in the encounter, shall bruise the serpent's head. (Gen. iii. 15.) This is the figure by which our Lord first illustrates the effect of His death. The Good Shepherd lays down his life for the sheep in doing battle with the beast of prey who would ravage the flock. (John x. 11.) There is no idea here of paying a penalty to God, as if His anger had to be bought off. Nor is there any idea of paying a ransom to Satan, as if he had any rights over fallen man. This is a grotesque caricature of the truth that Satan, the prince of this world, held men in his grasp, from which they were delivered by the moral victory of Christ's perfect obedience in spite of every seduction and of every assault. The prince of this world came to Christ and tested Him in what we call specifically the Temptation and in the Passion; but found nothing in Him on which he could lay hold, nothing inconsistent with absolute love and loyalty to the Father. (John xiv. 30.)[5] He was obedient to death, even to the surrender of His life, and that on the cross. (Phil. ii. 8; John xii. 31.)

---

[5] See the last of the author's Baldwin Lectures, *Christ's Temptation and Ours*.

THE ATONEMENT

Thus was the prince of this world cast out. Christ is represented in His passion as wrestling with spiritual foes. He puts off from Himself the temptations by which they would ensnare, the bands by which they seek to hold Him. So on and by the cross He triumphs over them and displays them as His captives. (Col. ii. 15.)[6]

In this sense we are said to be *purchased* by Christ, bought, that is, at cost, *from* the power of Satan, from an evil life, from indifference and self-love, *for* His service, in which we shall find our true freedom, that He may use us for His purposes. (*e. g.* Tit. ii. 14; Rev. v. 9; 1 Cor. vi. 20.)

4. *Christ offers a perfect satisfaction or reparation for sin.*—"He is the propitation for our sins; and not for ours only, but also for the whole world" (1 John ii. 2).[7] To propitiate is to render propitious or favorable. With reference to God's regard of man this is effected chiefly by the removing of that which necessarily causes displeasure. A holy being must abhor that which is contrary to his own nature. So long and so far as man clings to that which is evil, he

---

[6] Note the three verbs:

ἀπεκδυσάμενος, He stripped off from Himself, by wresting freed Himself.

ἐδειγμάτισεν, like a conquerer returning in triumph, H displays the captives, the trophies He has won.

θριαμβεύσας, He leads them in the triumphal procession. "The paradox of the crucifixion is placed in the strongest light—triumph in helplessness and glory in shame. The convict's gibbet is the victor's car."—(Lightfoot *in loc.*)

[7] See Westcott's note *in loc.*

must be under the divine displeasure. Christ by His passion and obedience unto death delivers man from evil, and so reconciles him to God. The Lamb of God *takes away* the sin of the world.

At the same time, as the representative of mankind, He offers a reparation to God for the sins and offenses by which His holiness has been violated. If such a reparation be not a requirement of divine justice, it certainly is an instinct of the human heart, which would find its perfect expression in the Son of man. In the case of one whom we may have injured or pained, we are not content with amending our conduct for the future, nor simply with an apology in words. We desire, if possible, to make what amends we can, to *manifest* our sorrow, and hence we would gladly suffer in the other's service, to prove our change of mind. Even so Christ on our behalf endured pain and humiliation and death, not as a penalty imposed upon Him by God, but as a protestation of His love for His Father above all things, and of His grief at the offenses against His Father committed by men in preferring to Him pleasure and gain and honor.

By the offering of such a reparation it may have been made possible for God to forgive man freely without exposing Himself to misunderstanding as thinking lightly of sin, or lowering the standard of holiness. (Comp. Rom. iii. 24-26.)

5. The Atonement (as a reparation, a deliverance, a purchase, an exhibition of God's love, and of man's true character) is spoken of as *effected by Christ's Blood*. We must guard here against any unworthy and materialistic ideas. Blood in Holy Scripture is

the constant symbol of life. Blood shed stands for life laid down; blood sprinkled for life imparted. Christ's blood is shed for us, in that His life is surrendered in obedience unto death. His blood is sprinkled on us, in that by the Holy Spirit, and especially in the Sacraments of Baptism and Holy Communion, we are made partakers of His glorified humanity which was perfected through suffering.[8]

Symbolism of the Levitical Sacrifices.— We may note some leading points in the symbolism of the Levitical Sacrifices, and the light they throw on our Lord's Sacrifice, in which they found their realization:[9]

1. That which was offered (whether an animal victim or an offering of the fruits of the earth) was given to God as a symbol of the personal and moral surrender of the offerer, whether an individual or the people as a whole.

2. In the case of an animal victim, it was not the mere death that constituted the offering; it was the blood which had passed through death which was offered to God, representing the life broken away from this lower world. This, offered on the altar, was said to 'cover' the disobediences of the people.

3. In certain cases, as of purification, a portion of the blood was sprinkled on the offerer, representing the impartation to him of a new life accepted by God, to purge away the old defilement.

---
[8] See note on the significance of the Blood of Christ in Westcott, *The Epistles of St. John*, p. 34 ff.
[9] See E. F. Willis, *Worship of the Old Covenant;* W. P. DuBose, *Soteriology*.

4. The other features of sacrifice led up to the sacrificial meal, in which the worshipper partook of that which had been accepted by God, and so was made a guest at His table. This fellowship (at-one-ment) with God was the end of sacrifice.

These further points should be kept in mind in order to guard against unworthy notions of our Lord's Sacrifice:

1. As has been insisted on in the chapter on the Trinity, there is no division of attributes, or difference of character, between the Father and the Son. The holiness which required the sacrifice was the holiness of the Son as of the Father: the love which provided the sacrifice was the love of the Father as of the Son.

2. Christ is not our Substitute, but our Leader and Representative: (a) He is not *a* man, an individual member of the race, but the Son of man, the representative of the race; (b) He did for us what, without His aid, we could never have attempted; but now, if we would benefit by what He has done for us, we must share in it. We are baptized into His death. We must continually mortify all our evil and corrupt desires. His death and resurrection *for* us must be reproduced *in* us.

3. Scripture constantly affirms that Christ 'bore our sins;' but that He 'bore the punishment of our sins,' never. To the consequences of our sins He voluntarily submitted Himself, that He might fight out our battle, and hallow all our experiences by His sympathy and example.

4. He offered to God no external oblation, but Himself, in absolute and perfect correspondence with His Father's will. This is the essence of all acceptable sacrifice, "Lo, I come to do Thy will, O God" (Heb. x. 5-10). It is this which we proclaim and plead in the Eucharist (1 Cor. xi. 26), His obedience unto death; it is this which we are pledged to reproduce, in our lives, offering to God ourselves, our souls and bodies, as a reasonable, holy and living sacrifice (Rom. xii. 1).

5. To guard against a one-sided view of Christ's Passion, it is well to remember that —

(1) He died *by* sin, at the hands of sin. This is the historical view of the Passion, given in the Gospel narratives, the basis of all further theological and spiritual explanation, both in our Lord's teaching and that of His apostles, and in the prophecies and types of the Old Testament. Envy, hatred, worldliness, covetousness, sensuality and cowardice combined to put Jesus to death.

(2) He died *for* sin :
  (a) in general, to secure forgiveness and make reconciliation;
  (b) in particular, offering reparation and satisfaction for our offenses. (See p. 89.)

(3) He died *to* or *from* sin, separating Himself entirely from its entanglements. (Rom. vi. 1-14.) Thus the external physical death was the expression of the inner repudiation of all that would hinder perfect obedience and love to God.

BIBLIOGRAPHY

Leighton Pullan, "The Atonement." (Oxford Library of Practical Theology.)

A. C. A. Hall, "The Forgiveness of Sins." (Sermon III., Our Lord's Sacrifice the ground of Forgiveness.)

A. C. A. Hall, "Christ's Temptation and Ours." (Baldwin Lectures, 1896), Lect. VI.

H. N. Oxenham, "The Catholic Doctrine of the Atonement."

J. McLeod Campbell, "The Nature of the Atonement."

W. P. DuBose, "Soteriology of the New Testament."

W. P. DuBose, "The Gospel according to St. Paul."

W. H. Hutchings, "Some aspects of the Cross."

W. O. Burrows, "The Mystery of the Cross."

R. W. Dale, "The Atonement."

J. H. Beibitz, *Gloria Crucis*.

A. Lyttleton, "The Atonement" (in *Lux Mundi*).

Sanday and Headlam, "The Epistle to the Romans," p. 91 ff.

C. Gore, "Epistle to the Romans."

C. Gore, "The New Theology and the Old Religion." (Lect. IV., The idea of Sin; VII., The Atonement; Sermon III., The Christian idea of Sin.)

G. Bull, "The State of man before the Fall."

G. H. Curteis, "Scientific Obstacles to Christian Belief." (Boyle Lectures, 1888. Lect. V. and VI., The Fall and Redemption.)

R. C. Moberly, "Personality and Atonement."

J. M. Wilson, "The Gospel of the Atonement." (Hulsean Lectures, 1898.)

H. C. Beeching, "The Bible doctrine of Atonement."

E. Griffith-Jones, "Ascent through Christ." (Bk. I, cc. iv., v., vi., vii.)

I. A. Dorner, "System of Christian Doctrine." (Vol. II, part ii. § 71 ff.)

VI.

THE RESURRECTION

Meaning of the Descent into Hades.— The descent into Hades is emphasized in the Creed as witnessing to the reality and integrity of Christ's manhood, and so to His perfect sympathy with us in all the experiences of life. (By Hades or Hell is meant, of course, the common abode of departed spirits, and not Gehenna the place of punishment for the guilty.) "He has won for God and hallowed every condition of human existence. We cannot be where He has not been. He bore our nature as living: He bore our nature as dead."—(Westcott, *Historic Faith*, p. 77.)

The vital and the personal union in Christ.—Death was to Christ, as to all men, the severance of the vital union between soul and body. His body was laid in the grave; His soul went into the world of spirits. The resurrection was the restoration of the vital union between soul and body, so that He lived again in the integrity of human nature. Meanwhile the personal or hypostatic union, whereby His human nature was joined to the divine in His single person, was never severed. The body in the sepulchre was the human body of the eternal Son of God; the soul in Hades was the human soul of the eternal Son of God.

Christ's disembodied soul not inactive.—The soul of Christ was not unconscious or inactive in the spirit world. "Being put to death in the flesh, but quickened by the spirit, ... He went and preached unto the spirits in prison" (1 Pet. iii. 18-20). Concerning this passage, and hence throughout his treatment of this article of the Creed, Pearson is misled by the undoubtedly wrong reading τῷ πνεύματι, which he understands to refer to the Holy Ghost: but σαρκὶ and πνεύματι (both without the article) are contrasted as the physical and the spiritual elements of man's nature, his body and soul.

The spirits in prison mentioned by S. Peter are those who were once disobedient in the days of Noah, not heeding his warnings of the coming flood, by which, as a temporal punishment, they were destroyed. To such Christ proclaimed the deliverance He had wrought, the forgiveness He had won for all true penitents by His cross and passion.

The Resurrection a sign repeatedly promised.— The Resurrection was the sign repeatedly promised by our Lord as a proof that His claims were true. When having been put to an ignominious death He was raised to life again, this would be an attestation that He was all He claimed to be, a messenger from God, the promised Messiah, God's Son in an altogether unique sense. Born of the seed of David according to the flesh, He was declared to be (marked out as) the Son of God with power, according to the spirit of holiness (His divine nature) by the resurrection from the dead. (Rom. i. 4; Matt. xii. 38-40, xvi. 4; Mark x. 32-34; John ii. 18-22.)

And continually pressed by the apostles.—Accordingly it was on the fact of the resurrection that the apostles based their teaching. They consistently preached "Jesus and the resurrection." (*e. g.* S. Peter, Acts i. 22, iv. 33, x. 41, etc.; S. Paul, Acts xvii. 18, 31; 1 Cor. xv. 1-17.)

It was this fact which had wrought the great change in the disciples' own attitude and temper. It was this to which they appealed in preaching both to Jews and to Gentiles.

This sign involved a *real* resurrection. Immortality of influence or continued bodiless existence would give no such attestation. A restoration to the integrity of human life, physical as well as spiritual, was required, and it is to this that the apostles bore witness. They saw their Master, they conversed with Him, He ate before them; in spite of their misgivings and doubts He convinced them of His identity by voice and manner and by the woundprints in His hands and feet. (Acts x. 41; Luke xxiv. 30, 31; John xxi. 13.)

The Resurrection not a return to former conditions.— At the same time the resurrection was not a return to the old conditions of life. This idea is wholly excluded both by the narratives of the risen life and by the apostles' comments thereon. What is clear is that the sepulchre on Easter morning was found empty. The Lord had risen. No one ever pretended to have seen Him rise. The body that had been laid in the grave had been re-assumed by the spirit in a new mode of existence. He passed through the closed door, He appeared and disappeared as He pleased, and in different forms according to the occasion. His body was now a spiritual body, σῶμα πνευματικόν. Freed from former limitations, and entirely under the control of the indwelling spirit, it no longer belonged to this lower sphere, while yet capable of being manifested to the senses.

Difference between Christ's resurrection and such as had been before.— Thus Christ was the "first-fruits of them that slept" (1 Cor. xv. 20). Others had been called back to the old life. Not to mention instances in the Old Testament Scriptures, our Lord during His ministry had raised from the dead the daughter of Jairus, the son of the widow of Nain, and Lazarus. (Mark v. 21-43; Luke vii. 11-17; John xi.) But in these cases there was only a relaxation of the grasp of death. The person returned to the old conditions. He was still subject to death. Christ rose to a new kind of life, over which death had no power.

The Resurrection "according to the Scriptures."— In the Creed, as by St. Paul, Christ is said to have been raised again "according to the Scriptures." And our Lord Himself shewed His disciples from the Law, the Prophets, and the Psalms (the three divisions of the Old Testament Scriptures) that it was necessary that the Christ should suffer and rise again (Luke xxiv. 27, 44-46). The reference probably is not only to particular texts and predictions, such as Ps. xvi. 8 (cited by S. Peter, Acts ii. 25), Hos. xiii. 14, and Isa. liii, but also to the whole record of God's dealing with His people, collectively and individually, in which

He is continually seen bringing good out of evil, life out of death, construction out of dissolution. This law is specially illustrated in the deliverance of Israel from bondage in Egypt, and later from captivity in Babylon, and in the histories of Isaac, Joseph, David, Daniel, Jonah. All these experiences of God's servants would be recapitulated in the Messiah, as the great Representative of His people and of the race.

Purposes of the appearances of the risen Lord.—
Our Lord's appearances during the forty days between His resurrection and His ascension we may regard as intended—

(1) to convince the disciples of the truth of His resurrection;

(2) to wean them from reliance on His sensible manifestation, while assuring them of His being continually present, though unseen, and always ready to intervene on their behalf;

(3) to give the great commissions to the apostles, whereby the virtue of His death should be continually applied to men.

Having died to sin and having been perfected through suffering, He became the author of eternal salvation to all them that obey Him. (Rom. vi. 10; 1 Pet. ii. 24; Heb. v. 9.)[1]

The Ascension.—The Ascension is the perfecting of the Resurrection. Christ's risen body no longer be-

---

[1] See note on the "The Place of the Resurrection of Christ in the teaching of St. Paul," in Sanday and Headlam on **Romans**, p. 116 ff.

longed to this lower world. The greater part of His life after the resurrection was "hid with God." He came forth and manifested Himself to His disciples for special purposes from time to time during that period. When these purposes were accomplished, He finally withdrew from their sensible cognizance.

What change the "receiving up into heaven" may signify, we cannot tell. It is the figure used to express the raising of Christ's manhood to the glory which ever belonged to His divine person.

The Ascension marks the exaltation of our Lord in His manhood above all created beings; angels and authorities and powers are made subject unto Him. But it would be an error, confounding the manhood with the Godhead, to ascribe ubiquity to Christ's glorified humanity.

The Session.—At the Ascension Christ retained in spiritualized and glorified form the human nature which He had assumed. Presenting it, perfected through suffering, before God, He fulfilled the types of the ancient sacrifices, in which the blood of the victims was offered to God, symbolizing the life that had passed through death. So Christ, our great high priest, entered within the veil and presented Himself before God on our behalf, as our representative. Human nature in His person is seen perfectly corresponding with God's design for man. Thus exalted in our nature Christ ever lives to make intercession on our behalf. His presence as the Son of man at the right hand of God is the pledge that human needs are understood in heaven. His humanity is made the channel for the communication of divine gifts to men. As the Head of all He received gifts for men, and distributes these gifts to His people according to their several needs. These gifts are all summed up in the gift of the Holy Spirit, imparted from the glorified Head to the members of His mystical body. By His Spirit He is present with His people for spiritual purposes, meeting them in prayer and sacrament. His removal from our sensible cognizance, in a presence circumscribed by conditions of time and space, was a necessary condition for this higher and spiritual presence. (Comp. John xvi, 7.)

The Return to Judgment.—We are taught to look for a manifestation of Christ at the end of this present age. In glorious majesty the Redeemer will appear as the Judge of all. This will be the culmination of many judgments, or crises, in which the sovereignty of the Son of man has been progressively manifested. In particular the Fall of Jerusalem, which meant the entire ending of the Jewish dispensation and the establishment of the Christian Church as God's representative in this world, was spoken of by our Lord as a figure of the final judgment, and of the establishment of His kingdom upon the overthrow of all opposing forces.

God has appointed a day in which He will judge the world by that Man whom He has ordained. Christ's coming to judge with the Father's authority will be the final act in the vindication of Him who was unjustly condemned and despised, a symbol of the reversal of human judgments in that day. In part the manifestation of the Son of man *will be the judgment*. By their likeness or unlikeness to Him, the pattern of the race, men will be judged, and by the use which they have made of the victory He has won on their behalf, and of the help which He has offered them.

BIBLIOGRAPHY

W. J. Sparrow Simpson, "Our Lord's Resurrection." (Oxford Library of Practical Theology.)

H. B. Swete, "The Appearances of our Lord after the Passion."

W. Milligan, "The Resurrection of our Lord."

W. Milligan, "The Ascension and Heavenly Priesthood."

B. F. Westcott, "The Gospel of the Resurrection."

B. F. Westcott, "The Revelation of the Risen Lord."

H. Latham, "The Risen Master."

H. P. Liddon, "Easter at St. Paul's."

E. H. Plumptre, "The Spirits in Prison."

E. Griffith-Jones, "Ascent through Christ," Bk. III., cc. i and ii.

A. B. Bruce, "Apologetics," Bk. III.

Charles Harris, "Pro Fide," ch. xxii.

W. H. Turton, "The Truth of Christianity," Pt. III., ch. xvii.

VII.

THE HOLY GHOST

Relation of the Spirit's work to that of Christ.—
The Trinity in its relation to us may be expressed
thus: the Father is *God in His infinite Being*,
"whom no man hath seen, nor can see." (1 Tim.
vi. 16.) The Son, Jesus Christ, is *God as man*, the
Word made flesh, acting out God's true character
before our eyes, in our nature and amid our experiences, showing us at once what God is, and
what man made in God's image should be, and may
by His help become.[1] (John i. 18.) The Holy Spirit
is *God in men and women*, reproducing by degrees *in* Christ's disciples the perfect pattern that
has been given *to* us by Christ. The same perfect
holiness, truth, purity, and love that we worship in
God, and that was manifested in the human life and
work of Jesus Christ, is communicated to us by
the Holy Spirit, making us partakers of the divine
nature. (2 Pet. i. 4.)

The Word of God approaches us from *without*, and
gives an external objective revelation; the work of
the Spirit is *within* and subjective, acting upon our

---

[1] "What Christ effected in the world of history, the
Spirit inwardly appropriates and brings into the inner world
of the human soul; this has been the office of the Spirit of God
from the beginning."—(Luthardt, *Saving Truths of Christianity*, p. 177.)

106   THE DOCTRINE OF THE CHURCH

own faculties, and enabling them to correspond with the external revelation.[2] (Eph. i. 18.)

Thus we see the meaning of the title 'Spirit,' as given to the third person of the Trinity. The Divine Being is Spirit. That describes His nature. (John iv. 24.) The poverty of language compels us to use the same word to express the going forth of the divine activity.[3] This we recognize in the love of the Father for the Son, returned by the Son to the Father (in this sense the Spirit is spoken of as the Bond of the eternal Trinity),[4] and in the communication of divine life to created beings.

The Giver of Life.—The Holy Spirit is spoken of in the Nicene Creed as the Life-giver. From the beginning this has been His office — to communicate from God life to the world.

Physical life is a sharing of the life which is in God. Intellectual, rational life is a further sharing of His life. Moral and spiritual life makes man God's son in a higher sense than any lower creature. Christ came to restore man's divine sonship, that man might have life, and have it more freely and richly. (John x. 10.)

---

[2] In English the older word 'Ghost' is in this application exactly equivalent to 'Spirit,' but probably to most persons it suggests a somewhat more *personal* idea than belongs to Spirit.

[3] See *Elements of Christian Doctrine*, by T. A. Lacey (p. 177), who quotes S. Thomas Aquinas: "*Quo nomine quaedam vitalis motio et impulsio designatur; prout aliquis ex amore dicitur moveri, vel impelli ad aliquid faciendum.*" (*Summa*, I. x.xvii. 4.)

[4] See Chapter III, p. 51.

This He accomplished (1) by hallowing our nature in His own person, through His own life of struggle and discipline, in which all His human faculties were continually under the control of the Spirit of God, and then (2) by breathing forth on His disciples the Spirit by which His human nature had been sanctified. So He imparted to them the life of God which had been manifested in the flesh in His earthly experience. (1 John i. 1, 2; 1 Tim. iii. 16.)

This gift of holiness (described as love and light), the highest degree of God's life that is conceivable, does not obliterate our personality. It is the communication of God's life to us, rather than the absorption of our life in God. The natural faculties with which we are endowed, our memory, our reason, our affections, our conscience, and our will, are raised by the life-giving Spirit of God to a higher energy; we are enabled to become our best selves.[5]

Something has already been said in the chapter on the Trinity about our Lord's teaching concerning the Holy Spirit, and of the apostles' understanding thereof as shown in their writings. Some other passages of Scripture treating of the Spirit may be cited, which will show (1) His Deity, (2) His distinct Personality, (3) His interior operation (see above, p. 105), and (4) the association of His operation with that of the Word or Son of God.

1. *The Deity of the Spirit.*—The Godhead of the Spirit is plainly implied by our Lord's warning that

---

[5] "All the life of God in us is nothing except as it is all our own freedom, all our own selves, all our own activity and life in God."—(DuBose, *High Priesthood and Sacrifice*, p. 219.)

blasphemy against the Spirit hath never forgiveness (Mark iii. 29), and by S. Paul's teaching that by His indwelling He makes our souls and bodies temples of God (1 Cor. iii. 16, vi. 19), while S. Peter distinctly says that to lie to the Holy Ghost is to lie to God (Acts v. 3, 4).

2. *His distinct Personality.*— That the Spirit of God is no mere impersonal attribute or influence, is shown by our Lord's designation of Him as another Helper (παράκλητος, a personal title) to take His place (John xiv. 16-26), and by His attributing to Him personal actions, as teaching, guiding, reminding, bearing witness. He can be grieved (Eph. iv. 30); He distributes gifts and is expressly distinguished from the gifts which he distributes (1 Cor. xii. 4-11).[6] In S. Paul's description of the Spirit's intercession He is plainly distinct from the Father with whom He intercedes, and from us for whom he pleads (Rom. viii. 26, 27).[7]

3. *His interior operation.*— As has been said, the operation of the Spirit is *within*, enabling the creature to correspond with the call of the Word of God. This would seem to be the Spirit's function in nature; this was His part in the Incarnation — (1) quickening

---

[6] While the same term, πνεῦμα, is used both for the Person and His gift, as a rule (though not an invariable rule outside S. John's writings) the presence of the article, τὸ πνεῦμα, marks the divine Person, while the noun without the article stands for His gift or influence.

[7] The use of the masculine pronoun ἐκεῖνος in St. John xiv. 26 is emphatic.

the powers of the Virgin mother (Luke i. 35), (2) anointing the sacred manhood of our Lord for His life and work (Luke iii. 22, iv. 1; John i.33; Acts x. 38; Heb. ix. 14). In like manner He "spake by (διά) the prophets," quickening their powers both of insight and of proclamation (2 Pet. i. 21).[8] So by His inspiration He leads us into all truth of faith and of life, He aids us in prayer, kindling our affections towards God, and suggesting the petitions which God will be pleased to hear (Rom. viii. 20, 27, v. 5).

4 *The Spirit of Christ.*— In all He works with the Son of God. As by the Spirit of God Christ casts out demons (Matt. xii. 28), so it is the Spirit's function to take of the things of Christ and impart them to us. (John xvi. 14.)[9] He is "the Spirit of Christ" coming to us through the manhood of

---

[8]"The prophets in Israel were men specially illuminated by the Holy Ghost, men who had a peculiar insight into the counsels of God. This knowledge enabled them to predict. Enlightened by the revelation they saw the true drift of things, as it were, from the point of view of God; they saw what a crisis demanded, how it looked in the spiritual world. . . . Thus prophets were men of their age. They looked upon the life around them with a gaze quickened by the inspiration of God, and they read off from it the laws of God's Providence, and predicted on its basis that which was to come. We rarely, if ever, find them speaking from a historic standpoint not their own."—(Strong's *Manual of Theology*, p. 277.)

[9]" From the Father, by the Son, through the Spirit, all things are. That which the Son doth hear of the Father, and which the Spirit doth receive of the Father and the Son, the same we have at the hands of the Spirit as being the last, and therefore the nearest unto us in order, although in power the same with the second and the first."—(Hooker, *Eccl. Pol.* I. li. 2.)

Christ which He has hallowed, in which His holiness has been manifested.

The Lord and Life-giver.— The distinct enunciation of what had always been the Church's implicit faith with regard to the Spirit of God, was called forth, like the explicit declaration of her faith in the Incarnation of the Son of God, by denials of the truth. In repelling false notions the faithful came to a clearer understanding and expression of their belief. So it was that when in the middle of the fourth century Macedonius and his followers taught of the Holy Spirit, as Arius had taught of the Son, that He was a creature (κτίσμα) of God, there was added to the existing profession of belief "in the Holy Ghost" (which was all the Creed of Nicea affirmed), the further words declaring Him to be "the Lord and the Life-giver, (τὸ κύριον καὶ τὸ ζωοποιόν), who proceedeth from the Father, who with the Father and the Son is worshipped and glorified, who spake by the prophets."[10]

The Single or Double Procession.— The controversy concerning the *Filioque,* or the Double Procession of the Holy Spirit from the Father *and the Son,* is largely a matter of ecclesiastical history. It must be admitted that the clause was introduced into the

---

[10] This addition to the Nicene creed (proper) is first found in a creed given by Epiphanius (*Ancoratus,* § 118) in 374. It was perhaps sanctioned by the Council of Constantinople (381), which condemned the heresy against which the words were a protest; in any case the Creed containing the addition was recognized by the Council of Chalcedon (451).

Creed without proper authority, the Western Church having no right to amend a Confession of Faith that belongs to the whole Church, without the assent of Eastern Christendom. Moreover, the action of the Western Church may be considered irregular, in that it was taken by no council, but by papal authority, and that largely under the pressure of secular sovereigns. On the doctrinal side divergence may have been partly due to a difference between the Greek word, ἐκπορεύεσθαι, (which was understood as meaning to go forth as from a source) and the Latin, *procedere*, (which simply indicates going forth, without necessarily involving any idea of origin). Eastern theologians are bent on preserving the single source (πηγή, ἀρχή) of deity, which Western divines also recognize. (ch. III, p. 51.) The Son derives His being from the Father; so does the Holy Spirit. But since the Son is the express image of the Father, it is argued that the Son must have a share in the communication of life and being to the Spirit. It must, of course, be kept in mind that there is no question of priority in time, only of order and thought, with regard to the mutual relation of the Persons of the Trinity. God exists always, eternally, in a three-fold manner. So understood there is no impossibility of reconciliation between Eastern and Western doctrinal positions. The East would recognize not only a temporal mission of the Spirit from the exalted Christ, but also such an eternal procession from the Son as did not interfere with the acceptance of the Father as the single fount of the divine life.[11]

Passages of Scripture may be cited on either side; but they can be harmonized in the light of what has been said; *e. g.*

> the Spirit proceeds from the Father (John xv. 26), from the throne of God and of the Lamb (Rev. xxii. 1);
> He is sent by the Son (John xv. 26),
> He is called the Spirit of Christ (Rom. viii. 9; Phil. i. 19; 1 Pet. i. 11; Gal. iv. 6).

The operation of the Spirit of God on the spirit of man we call Grace. The word Grace comes to have this meaning by three steps: (1) Originally the word means favor, the good will which God has for His people. But God's good will is never sentimental; His favor is not inoperative. His mercy comes forth to supply the needs which He sees. So (2) Grace stands for any gift, spiritual or temporal, which God freely gives us of His bounty; and (3) in particular the gift of spiritual aid which He bestows on us to enable us to live aright and attain our final

---

[11] "It is of great importance to insist that there is no radical dogmatic difference on this point between the Eastern and the Western Churches. Both held precisely the same beliefs, and hold them still; but they describe them in different ways. And a point like this could hardly have been a subject upon which two churches could have suspended communion, if it had not been for the rancour which political disputes imparted to the discussion."—(Strong, *Manual of Theology*, p. 172; Comp. Stone, *Outlines of Christian Dogma*, pp. 28, 29; Lias, *The Nicene Creed*, pp. 254-263. Swete, *History of the Doctrine of the Procession of the Holy Spirit.*)

blessedness. Of this aid man would stand in need were his nature unfallen, in order that he might attain his true end of fellowship with God. Still more in our disordered condition are we dependent for guidance and self-control on the grace of God. It is important to remember amid the frequent use of the word, in various technical phrases, that Grace is no abstract spiritual force, like electricity in the atmosphere, to be captured and applied. It is nothing else than the touch of the Spirit of God on the spirit of man; the touch of the Spirit of love and truth and purity, to enlighten our reason, to quicken our conscience, to purify and expand our affections, and to strengthen our will.

It follows that Grace requires our coöperation. It is never irresistible. The Spirit of God may be "grieved" or even "quenched." We are to work out our own salvation with fear and trembling, because it is God who worketh in us. (Phil. ii. 12.) So S. Paul describes the work of grace in his own experience: By the grace [or help] of God I am what I am; and His grace [or help] which was bestowed upon me was not found vain [it was not fruitless, but accomplished its intended purpose]; but I laboured more abundantly than they all [the other apostles]; yet not I [of my own initiation or strength], but the grace [or help] of God which was with me [prompting and enabling me.] (1 Cor. xv. 10.)

The Paraclete.— Grace is spiritual help. The Spirit of God is given to strengthen us with power in the inward man. (Eph. iii. 16.) Here we see the meaning of the title by which our Lord constantly described the Holy Spirit whom He promised to send —"the Paraclete." (John xiv. 16, 17, 26, xv. 26, xvi. 7.) The Greek word means quite literally one who is called to our side to help us in any difficulty. In the margin of the Revised Version of the New Testament the word 'Helper' is given as an alternative for 'Comforter,' and for a single word this is probably the best to express the sense of the original.

BIBLIOGRAPHY

J. C. Hare, "The Mission of the Comforter."

J. E. C. Welldon, "The Revelation of the Holy Spirit."

W. H. Hutchings, "The Person and Work of the Holy Ghost."

A. C. A. Hall, "The Work of the Holy Spirit, illustrated by New Testament Symbols."

R. C. Moberly, "Atonement and Personality," cc. VIII and IX.

C. A. Swainson, "The Doctrine of the Holy Spirit."

H. B. Swete, "The History of the Doctrine of the Procession of the Holy Spirit."

R. W. Dale, "Christian Doctrine," ch. VI, The Holy Spirit.

J. F. Bethune-Baker, "Introduction to the Early History of Christian Doctrine," ch. VIII.

VIII.

THE CHURCH

The Church corresponds with man's social being.—
Man is created a social being, having relations with
his fellows. He is dependent on them for the full development and exercise of his powers. As civiliza-
tion advances, this becomes the more evident. No
one is sufficient unto himself. (Gen. ii. 18.)[1]

The same law applies to man's regenerate life.
Christ came not to call individual disciples to follow
Him in isolation. He formed His disciples into a
society which He called His Church. (Matt. xvi. 18,
19, xviii. 15-18.) This Christian society succeeded
to the prerogatives of the Jewish Church as God's
chosen people and His authoritative representative
in the world. But it differs in two respects from the
Jewish Church: (1) The Christian Church is
catholic, universal, gathering men from all nations,
whereas the Jewish Church was national, limited
practically to the descendants of Jacob. (2) The
Christian Church is endowed with higher spiritual
gifts, with the presence of the Spirit of God, which
could not be bestowed until the redemption of man
had been wrought out. (John vii. 39.)

*Not a voluntary organization, but a spiritual or-
ganism.*— The Church according to God's design is

---

[1] Comp. Aristotle, *Pol.* I. 2, φύσει πολιτικὸν ζῶον.

not a voluntary organization which Christians may join or not, as they deem best for their own edification or for the service of others. It is the Body of Christ, the blessed company of all faithful people, to which we are joined when we are united with Christ by Baptism, and in which we are to be nourished and trained.

"Men were not brought to Christ and then determined that they would live in a community. Men were not brought to Christ to believe in Him and His Cross, and to recognize the duty of worshipping the Heavenly Father in His name, and then decided that it would be a great help to their religion that they should join one another in that worship, and should be united in the bonds of fellowship for that purpose. In the New Testament, on the contrary, the Kingdom of Heaven is already in existence, and men are invited into it. The Church takes its origin, not in the will of man, but in the will of the Lord Jesus Christ."— Abp. Temple, *Individualism and Catholicism*.[2]

Admission to the Church by Baptism.— We are admitted to the fellowship of the Church (a) on the promise on our part (explicit or implicit): (1) Of *Renunciation* of the Devil (under whose power we were born), the World, and the Flesh; (2) Of *Belief*

---

[2] Comp. Bp. Satterlee: "Observe that [the Kingdom of Heaven or the Church] was an organism, not an organization. This distinction is never to be lost sight of. An organization is a federation formed by men; an organism is a body endued with the power of life, and created by God."— (*New Testament Churchmanship*, p. 123.)

in Christ and His revelation; (3) Of *Obedience* to His commandments.

(b) We then receive the washing of regeneration and renewing of the Holy Ghost, the cleansing of the body by water being the symbol of the cleansing of our inner nature by the Spirit of God. With the forgiveness of sins is the communication of a new life, as we are made members of Christ, children of God, and inheritors of the Kingdom of Heaven. Our Baptism is "sealed," by a further gift of the Spirit to dwell in us, through the laying on of the hands of the Chief Pastor in Confirmation. This regenerate life is to be continually nourished by the spiritual food of Christ's body and blood in the Holy Communion.

The fellowship of the Church maintained in the Eucharist.— In the Eucharist, according to our Lord's command, we continually proclaim His death — that is, the moral victory of His obedience even to the laying down of His life. In this triumph of the Son of Man we glory and make our boast, and along with our praise and thanksgiving for the redemption He has won for all men, we claim our share in the benefits of His sacrifice by feeding upon the body which was given and the blood which was shed on our behalf.

Thus our union with our Lord is continually cemented; we draw into ourselves the virtue of His renewed humanity, and should grow into His likeness more and more. The Sacrament of our Lord's body and blood is the great pledge and symbol of the fellowship of His disciples one with another, as they are all made partakers of the one bread. The common life takes possession of all the members of the body. The celebration of the Holy Communion is accordingly the great central act of the Church's worship. With her sacrifice of praise and thanksgiving she offers in Christ's name her most solemn prayers and intercessions on behalf of all, pleading His merits whose death she shews in the memorial He Himself instituted.

The principle of Sacraments.— Sacraments are not charms, working with any magical effect. They are divinely ordained meeting-points with God, where He pledges to meet His people and bestow on them gifts of spiritual blessing, provided they approach His ordinance with right and fitting dispositions. The outward and visible sign is more than a condescension to our infirmity; it follows the analogy of the two-fold nature in which God made us, and the law of the Incarnation by which He restored our nature.

Man, with his material and spiritual being, is a sacrament; Christ, "God manifest in the flesh," is a sacrament; the special links between Christ and man, whereby He communicates His grace to us, are naturally sacramental. As in man, as in Christ, so in the Sacraments both parts, the outward and the inward, are equally real, each in its own sphere. It is not by our senses that we can lay hold of the inward part of a sacrament, but by faith, the action of our inner being. Baptism is the sacrament of new birth; by it we are made members of Christ. Holy Communion is the sacrament of spiritual nourishment; in it, by contact with Christ's renewed manhood, our regenerate life is continually strengthened.

Corresponding with the ideas of Birth and Nourishment a distinction is to be noted between Baptism and the Lord's Supper, which is recognized in the Catechism. In Baptism there are but two things to be considered:

(1) The outward, visible sign — water, wherein the person is baptized In the Name of the Father, and of the Son, and of the Holy Ghost;

(2) The inward spiritual grace — the death of the person unto sin, and his new birth unto righteousness.

In the Lord's Supper there are three things to be considered:

(1) The outward, visible sign — the bread and wine;

(2) The inward part or thing signified — the body and blood of Christ;

(3) The spiritual grace, or the benefits — the strengthening and refreshing of our souls by the body and blood of Christ, as our bodies are strengthened and refreshed by the bread and wine.

In Baptism the person is consecrated; new life is imparted directly to him. In Holy Communion the bread and wine are consecrated; spiritual food is provided which is then to be given to the communicant. The very idea of feeding, it must be remembered, involves spiritual activity on the part of the communicant, and not the mere passive reception of gifts of grace.[3]

The fellowship broken by sin.— The union with Christ by the gift of His Spirit, which it is the object of sacraments to form in the fellowship of the Church which is His body, is interrupted by sin. Any wilful violation of Christ's command, in the way of omission or of commission, involves a certain withdrawal from fellowship with Him. Grievous or persistent sin forfeits His presence. Yet not all sin is unto death. (1 John v. 17.) Upon true repentance sins may be forgiven and the penitent restored to the fellowship which had been forfeited. But the spiritual disease may be such that unaided its cure is well nigh impossible.

Spiritual discipline.— As we were admitted to the fellowship of the Church on the condition of our promise of conformity to the Christian standards, so our privileges in the Church are conditional on our loyalty to Christian faith and life. The Church may suspend, or even remove from her fellowship and privileges those who are guilty of grievous transgressions. Such discipline is exercised both for the benefit of the offender, that he may be won to repentance and a better mind, and also to preserve the Church

---

[3] To 'eat' and to 'drink' is to take in oneself by a voluntary act that which is without, and then to assimilate it and make it part of oneself. It is, as it were, faith regarded in its converse action. Faith throws the believer upon and into its object; this spiritual eating and drinking brings the object of faith into the believer."—(Westcott on St. John vi. 53.) This consideration explains and justifies the disuse of Infant Communion.

THE CHURCH

from contamination and laxity. On sufficient evidence of repentance, a person may be restored to his forfeited position in the Church.

Such disciplinary action is provided for by our Lord's warrant, and by the practice of the apostles. Christ gave to His Church not only the right but the duty to bind and to loose, *i. e.* to pass judgments as to what is to be permitted and what is not to be permitted in the Christian society (Matt. xviii. 15-18); and after His resurrection He gave the further power and duty to apply these judgments to persons, to absolve and to retain sins. (John xx. 23.) This power is chiefly exercised in admitting to or repelling from the Sacraments.

The exact rules for the exercise of spiritual discipline on these lines will be determined by ecclesiastical legislation, and will vary in details at different times and in different countries. It must always be remembered that in the exercise of discipline, perhaps even more than in the administration of the Sacraments, the bishop or priest acts, not in an isolated ministerial capacity, but as the president of the body as well as in the name of Christ. So St. Paul, in the exercise of discipline at Corinth, associated the local church with himself in both the exclusion and the reconciliation of the offender. (1 Cor. v. 3-11; 2 Cor. ii. 6-10.)

A distinction was made in early days between what was called the lesser and the greater excommunication. The former excluded persons from participation in the Eucharist, but did not expel them from the public prayers, in which, like the catechumens preparing for

Baptism, they were allowed to share in various degrees. By the greater excommunication, persons were wholly debarred from the society of the faithful — "not only excluded from communion in sacred things, but shunned and avoided in civil conversation as dangerous and infected persons."—(Bingham, *Christian Antiquities*, XVI, ii. 7, 8.)

This severer punishment would correspond with our Lord's words, "Let him be unto thee as an heathen man and a publican" (Matt. xviii. 17), and with St. Paul's, "With such an one, not even to eat" (1 Cor. v. 11). This was the delivering unto Satan for the destruction of the flesh, that the spirit might be saved in the day of the Lord Jesus; the withdrawal, that is, of the protection enjoyed by those who in the midst of an evil world are made citizens of the Kingdom of Heaven, and the surrender of them to the "prince of this world." (1 Cor. v. 5; 1 Tim. i. 20.) Our Lord Jesus Christ is, of course, the Supreme Authority, who annuls a sentence of remitting or retaining which is not according to His will. A further limitation must also be noted. A solemn excommunication, extending even to the denial of Christian rites at burial, is not to be regarded as a final sentence on the person's eternal condition. In such a case the Church leaves the person to God's judgment, to whom all is known, not having the evidence of repentance which would warrant her in pronouncing his reconciliation and restoration.

The Notes of the Church.— The Notes or marks of the Church are four. The Church is One, Holy,

Catholic, and Apostolic. These notes are characteristics of the Church's being, however sadly at different times they may be blurred as outward marks distinguishing the Church from other societies in the world. They should characterise her life and teaching and work.

1. The Church is *One*. There is one Body as there is One Spirit. (Eph. iv. 4.)

(a) This oneness is recognized by faith, as the Church is itself, in its spiritual character, an object of faith, although to natural sight it is but one among human societies. The unity of the Church is not something to be striven after, though it is to be realized more and more. It is because the Church is One Body, that Christians are bidden to live as befits that unity, to endeavor to preserve the unity of the Spirit in the bond of peace. Objective, spiritual unity should lead us to pray and work for the reunion of all Christian people in one visible body, that the Church may act with strength and decision. (John xvii. 22, 23.)

(b) Again, unity is quite distinct from union. There might be agreement among different bodies of Christians to act in concert; this would be union. The intended unity of the Church is something far beyond this; it is the assertion of one divine society, extending through the world, embracing persons of all ages and classes and nations and temperaments, with its confession and proclamation of one body of revealed truth, and its ministration by a divinely commissioned ministry of the same divinely appointed sacraments.

(c) This unity extends through all ages, as well as through all lands. That which really belongs to the Church's constitution, or to her faith, must be common to every age. That which was introduced at any date later than the time of the apostles cannot be an essential part of the deposit.

(d) This unity of the Body extends to the unseen world. All who have been duly baptized into Christ, and have not forfeited their position in Him, are members of the one Body, though they may no longer be in the flesh. The spiritual bonds which bind together those on earth, however scattered, bind together likewise those in Paradise with those on earth. Thus the Communion of Saints, the fellowship one with another of all the consecrated people of God, is another description of the Holy Catholic Church. The first clause speaks of the Christian society on its corporate side; the second (in apposition with the first) tells of the unity of the several members of the Body.

(e) It is the oneness of the Church, throughout the ages and throughout the world, which gives to her decisions their ultimate authority. A council of the Church does not derive its authority chiefly from the vote of the Bishops assembled. They bear testimony to what has been the Christian tradition in their several churches. And again the decision arrived at, if it is to be of lasting obligation, must commend itself to the Church generally. Thus it is recognized as the voice of the Spirit of God speaking in and through the Spirit-bearing Body of Christ.

In this light the authority of the Church is seen to be no arbitrary imposition of rules or doctrine on the body of believers by certain officers; it is rather the consent of the body at large on matters of grave importance, to which individuals bow.

2. The Church is *Holy* as the Body of Christ, in which the Holy Spirit dwells to lead its members into all truth, of life as well as of faith. (John xvi. 13.) The Greek word translated 'Holy' really means consecrated, rather than actually holy in inner experience. It was used of Israel as the consecrated people of God. To this position, with higher endowments, the Christian Church has succeeded. (Ex. xix. 6; 1 Pet. ii. 9.) The Communion of Saints is the fellowship of the consecrated servants of God, who indeed are called to be saints in the subjective sense.

As the realization of the note of Sanctity is marred by man's failure to correspond with God's design and to coöperate with His inspirations, so the note of Unity is likewise marred, and of necessity, since it is only in submission to the lordship of Christ and the rule of His Spirit that individual wilfulness can be controlled in humility and charity.

Our Lord's parables of the Tares and of the Dragnet prepare us for the presence within the Kingdom of those who do not really belong to it in spirit. (Matt. xiii.)

3. The Church is *Catholic*, as being intended to gather the elect from all nations and all classes. (Matt. xxviii. 19.) Each needs the truth and grace which are entrusted to the Church; and the Church

needs each. Each is to bring its special contribution to the common treasury, for the enrichment of the Church's thought, and the display of different virtues belonging to the Christian character. No chasm between different races, or sets of people, could be greater than that which existed between Jew and Gentile in apostolic times. The question of the Church's catholicity was threshed out in the controversy concerning the admission of Jew and Gentile into the Christian society on terms of perfect equality. In that fellowship "there can not be Greek and Jew, circumcision and uncircumcision, barbarian, Scythian, bondman, freeman; but Christ is all, and in all" (Col. iii. 11). The varieties of education and temperament and taste which mark the different members of the body of Christ are intended to have a mutually balancing and supplementing effect. At the same time they call for the exercise of mutual forbearance and a large-hearted generosity. This should be a characteristic of the Catholic Church.

4. The Church is *Apostolic*, as built upon the foundation of the apostles and prophets, from whom it received the treasures of truth and grace entrusted to them by Christ. The apostles were trained by our Lord during His earthly ministry, to act as His representatives when He should have left the earth, that He might work with them and through them. As the first Christians continued steadfastly in the apostles' teaching and fellowship, and in the breaking of bread, and in the prayers (Acts ii. 42), so all generations of Christendom were intended to be gathered round the ministry, inheriting authority from

the apostles, and to be held together by this chain running through all generations. The authority which the apostles received to act in Christ's name—beyond that which belonged to them as the original witnesses of His life and recipients of His revelation — was not a personal gift. It was transmitted to those who came into their place. God's gifts continue as long as the needs which they are intended to supply. "Therefore it is that the Christian ministry still includes in it the office of *teaching*, for education is necessary for every soul born into the world, and the office of *governing*, for decency and order are still necessary for the quiet and union of the Christian brotherhood. And so the office of applying the gifts of grace, the *priestly* office, is continued while there is guilt to be washed away, sinners to be reconconciled, believers to be strengthened, matured, comforted."—(J. H. Newman, *Parochial Sermons*, Vol. II, St. Peter's Day.)

The commissions which in the persons of the apostles the Church received to carry on Christ's work, to proclaim His truth to all nations, to win all to the obedience of the faith, constitute her His agent and representative on the earth. This is the function of the Body, to carry out the purposes of the Head. For this the Church is endowed with His Spirit.

The ministry an organ of the body.— The Church being one body has many members. There are various organs in the body, each having its special function to perform on behalf of the whole body. So it is with the ministry of the Christian Church. It exists not by itself nor for itself. Much confusion of thought would be avoided if this figure of the body were kept in mind. The body must have appropriate organs for the discharge of different functions. A living body does not create its own organs, nor substitute one for another. They are marked out from the beginning as parts of the living organism. The eye sees, the ear hears, the lips speak on behalf of the body, and with the power that comes from the common life of the body. So within the body of Christ there are orders of men marked out to whom the authority of government and ministry was committed by Christ. They are not external to the body, nor have they exclusive authority. Through them the Church acts.

Christ gave some to be apostles, and some prophets, and some evangelists, and some pastors and teachers, with a view to fitting the saints for the work of ministry for the building up of the body of Christ. (Eph. iv. 11, 12.)

These titles mark out different offices and kinds of service, general and local. From the apostles' time (*i. e.* at latest before St. John passed away), three permanent orders of ministers were recognized in the Church — Bishops, Presbyters, and Deacons. The Bishops alone had authority to ordain and commission others, who were chosen by the Church.

Transmission of the ministerial commission.— By such a ministerial succession a warrant and guarantee is provided for the administration of the Sacraments, which depend for their efficacy not on the individual minister's personal holiness or worthiness, but on the institution of Christ. When with right dispositions we approach His ordinances, He pledges Himself to bestow upon us the spiritual gift appropriate to each, *e. g.* cleansing and regeneration in Baptism, spiritual nourishment and refreshment in Holy Communion. With a ministry able to shew its continuity from those to whom Christ first gave His commission, we have a guarantee of validity, *i. e.* the security of His approval.[4]

The Catholic Church the elect body.— The Catholic Church is the elect body gathered out of all nations, as Israel of old was the chosen nation among all peoples; chosen to accomplish God's purpose, in bearing witness to Him before all. Such a choice is entirely in accordance with the general law of God's dealing, whereby some individuals or classes or nations are endued with special gifts to be used not merely for their own advantage, but on behalf of all. There is no idea of arbitrary favouritism, but rather of a responsible trusteeship, which must necessarily involve a stricter judgment. The conversion of the whole world to Christ is nowhere foretold; witness among all nations is the Church's duty.

Having considered the Church as the body of Christ, it is needful now to treat of the individual Christian's share in the privileges of the kingdom of

---

[4] This is the sense in which Ignatius uses the word 'valid' ($\beta\epsilon\beta a\iota a$), when he says, " Let that be counted a valid eucharist which is under the bishop or one to whom he has committed it." *Ad Smyrn.* § 8. We may well rejoice in this *security* of the Church's ministrations without presuming to pronounce any judgment upon the *efficacy* of other ministrations which have not the like guarantee.

heaven. The Church is the company of the elect, of those, that is, who are called by God and who correspond with His call. Why some should be within reach of the means of grace (which is more than a question of local contiguity) and others not, belongs to the secret things of God's Providence. This is clear, that *Election* is to grace and not to glory. Our final acceptance with God depends on our faithful and persevering correspondence with His grace. When a man corresponds with God's call, and by the aid of His Spirit submits himself to Christ in earnest repentance and faith, seeking His grace as He has promised to bestow it, he is justified; *i.e.* his past sins are pardoned for Christ's sake, with Whom he is now united, and from Whom he receives a gift of renewed spiritual life. This initial grace of regeneration, if diligently pursued and cultivated, will lead to a progressive sanctification, as the person's conduct and character are more and more controlled by the Spirit of God, and Christ's likeness is continually reproduced in His servant. This sanctification is the firstfruits of our final glorification, the earnest of our future inheritance. (Rom. viii. 30.)

BIBLIOGRAPHY

Dr. Hort, "The Christian Ecclesia."
W. Sanday, "The Conception of Priesthood."
Bishop Lightfoot, "The Christian Ministry" (in appendix to *Philippians*.)
G. Moberly, "The Administration of the Holy Spirit in the Body of Christ." (Bampton Lectures, 1868.)
W. Palmer, "The Church of Christ."
R. Field, "The Book of the Church."
A. Robertson, "*Regnum Dei*." (Bampton Lectures, 1901.)
C. Gore, "The Mission of the Church."
C. Gore, "Roman Catholic Claims" (especially cc. III and IV, on 'Authority').
E. Tyrrell Green, "The Church of Christ, her Mission, Sacraments and Discipline."
W. Lock, "The Church" (in *Lux Mundi*).
C. Gore, "The Church and the Ministry."
R. C. Moberly, "Ministerial Priesthood."
A. W. Haddan, "Apostolical Succession in the Church of England."

J. R. Illingworth, "Sacraments," ch. VIII. in "Christian Character."
F. Paget, "Sacraments" (in *Lux Mundi*).
R. I. Wilberforce, "The Doctrine of Holy Baptism."
Darwell Stone, "Holy Baptism." (Oxford Library of Practical Theology.)
A. J. Mason, "The Relation of Confirmation to Baptism."
A. C. A. Hall, "Confirmation." (Oxford Library of Practical Theology.)
C. Gore, "The Body of Christ."
Darwell Stone, "The Holy Communion."
F. Meyrick, "The Doctrine of the Holy Communion."

IX.

ESCHATOLOGY

Survival after death.— A continued existence after death, with a future recompense for conduct in this world, is not a distinctively Christian doctrine. It was held with various degrees of clearness by both Jews and heathen, and may be regarded as a human instinct asserting itself in spite of the pressure of the universal fact of death. It was generally in proportion as men rose to higher conceptions of human nature and its relation to God that they looked with confidence to the survival after death of the real self— that in us which thinks and remembers, which feels love and hate, joy and sorrow, hope and fear, that which chooses.[1] Where men have lived like beasts, they have been content to die like beasts. Those who have realized their higher powers, and in particular their capacity for communion with God, have clung to the assurance that He will not leave their souls in Hades, nor suffer them to perish. (Job xix. 25-27; Pss. xvi. 8-11, lxxiii. 23-26.) This expectation of future life is sanctioned and confirmed by Jesus Christ. Life, imperishable and incorruptible

---

[1] "Our moral feelings and emotions are not subject to deterioration or abatement with the lapse of years, down to the latest, in the same manner and degree as are the powers of memory, perception, reflexion."—(W. E. Gladstone, *Studies subsidiary to the works of Bishop Butler*, p. 150.)

life, is brought to light (2 Tim. i. 10.)[2] both by His teaching and especially by His resurrection, which shewed not only that man as a spiritual being survives death, but that his nature is to be restored to its integrity, physical and spiritual.[3]

The resurrection of the dead.— A resurrection, we are told, awaits all, both good and bad, that all may receive in the body a recompense for the things done in the body. (John v. 29; Acts xxiv. 15; 2 Cor. v. 10.) Man is by nature a composite being, with spiritual and material elements marvellously interwoven one with another. The disembodied spirit is not man in the integrity of his being. The very close and intimate connexion between soul and body, which science discloses and experience notes, may be thought to render probable (on the supposition of the soul's survival) a restoration of that union, the breaking of which in death seems so unnatural. "The body which has been so long the associate and partner of the soul's life, the instrument of its will, the minister of its passions, mingling lower physical sensations with that higher life of thought and feeling which belongs to it, could not be altogether cast away without impairing the completeness of our being,

---

[2] See Ellicott, *Pastoral Epistles, in loc.*, p. 116.

[3] On the Old Testament hope of immortality and the Christian doctrine, see Dr. Liddon's sermon, " Immortality," in his University Sermons, Series I, and the Appendix to Lecture V. in *The Christian View of God and of the World*, by James Orr, where it is contended that the Hebrew hope of future life was never limited to the immortality of the soul, but involved a restoration of the whole personality, in which the body too had a share.

without imperiling the continuous identity of our changeful existence."—(Liddon, *Some Elements of Religion*, p. 117. Comp. Westcott, *Historic Faith*, pp. 135, 136.)

This General Resurrection will be at the Last Day, at the manifestation of our Lord Jesus Christ. Of this and the subsequent judgment various figurative descriptions are given in the New Testament Scriptures. (Matt. xvi. 27, xxv. 31 *sq.*; John v. 27-29; 1 Thess. iv. 16, 17; Rev. i. 7, xx. 11, 12.) The chief points emphasized concerning the judgment are —

(a) the vindication of God's righteousness,
(b) the manifestation of all men as they truly are and have become,
(c) the bringing of all before the Son of man, Who is the Judge of all. (Rom. ii. 5; 2 Cor. v. 10; John v. 27.)

How this last Coming of Christ to judgment shall be accomplished which reveals the world to itself, we know not, and it is idle to speculate. (Westcott, *Historic Faith*, pp. 90, 91, 97.) Every manifestation of Christ involves a κρίσις. His last appearance will bring this world to a close, when final sentence will be pronounced on all.

Not a return to former conditions.—The resurrection will not be for us, any more than it was for our Lord Jesus Christ, a return to old conditions of bodily life. (See Chap. VI, p. 97.) Gross and crude ideas of a re-gathering and combining of the particles of which the body was composed are expressly excluded by St. Paul's teaching. "Flesh and blood," he says, "cannot inherit the kingdom of God, neither doth corruption inherit incorruption." (1 Cor. xv. 50.) Our bodies must be adapted to their new environment, transformed into the likeness of the Lord's risen body. (Phil. iii. 21.) The apostle illustrates the relation of the future body to the present body by the relation of a plant to its seed. (1 Cor. xv. 36-38.) The one is the real outcome of the other; it is not the restoration of the seed to its former condition. We do not expect at harvest time to receive back the seed which was put into the ground; we should be greatly disappointed if we received only this. We look for the waving ears that are the outcome of the seed.

By the "spiritual body," of which St. Paul speaks, is not to be understood (as some people imagine) a body composed of the thinnest kind of gaseous substance. (1 Cor. xv. 44.) A body made up of spirit would be a contradiction in terms. A spiritual body (σῶμα πνευματικόν) means rather a material body which is altogether under the dominion and control of our higher being which we call 'spirit,' corresponding to its needs, and having perhaps its character impressed upon it. The "natural body" (σῶμα ψυχικόν) is a body adapted to the mere life of nature, where the higher faculties have not been quickened by the touch of the Spirit of God. What the principle of unity, the connecting link between the present and the future body may be, we cannot tell, any more than we can exactly tell what binds together in one the constantly changing atoms of our present bodies, about the identity of which through different periods and stages of life we have no doubt.

The disembodied soul.— Meanwhile the disembodied soul retains a conscious existence. The term 'sleep,' used of death, applies to the body rather than to the soul. We may rather expect a quickening of the spiritual powers of memory, thought and affection, and an intensifying of their operations, when released from the burden of the flesh. When our Lord's human soul departed from the body it was not unconscious. Put to death in the flesh, He was quickened in the spirit, in which He went and preached unto the spirits in prison. (1 Pet. iii. 18, 19.) He promised to the penitent robber that he that very day should be with Him in Paradise. In His parable of Dives and Lazarus, neither were unconscious in the spirit world. (Luke xxiii. 43, xvi. 22-25.) St. Paul desired to depart and to be with Christ as being 'far better,' even when for him to live was Christ. It would be no gain for one whose life was lived in fellowship with Christ to be in His presence as an unconscious log. The departed, Christ said, speaking of the Old Testament patriarchs, "live unto God." (Luke xx. 38. Comp. 1 Pet. iv. 6.)

The intermediate state.— The condition of the faithful departed we may believe to be one of *progress*. Because probation is over, it by no means follows that education has ceased. They have not yet attained their perfection. The resurrection of the body ushers in the complete life of the world to come. Their full joy is to be attained when their nature is restored to its integrity, the body no longer being a clog upon the soul, but in its transfigured and spiritualized condition being made a fitting instrument for the soul's service of God. Meanwhile, freed from the distractions of the world as well as from the burden of the corruptible flesh, the spirit learns to see things as they really are. In the nearer presence of God there must be a growing desire for all good things, a reaching out more and more after Him in Whom is all goodness. At the same time, as the spirit reviews the past in the light of God and judges itself by true standards, there will be deepened penitence, and in deepened penitence increasing purification. As we follow the departed with our thoughts, we may offer prayers for their perfecting as well as thanksgiving for all that God has done for them. We may commend them continually to God's loving care and protection, and ask Him to supply their needs as He sees and knows them, and to lead them on in His knowledge and love in whatever way He wills. For such prayers we have the sanction of the early liturgies of the Church, which ask for the departed a continual increase of peace and rest and light, a merciful judgment at the Last Day, and a joyful welcome into the heavenly kingdom.[3]

---

[3] It may be sufficient to quote one such prayer, from the Liturgy of St. James: "Remember, O Lord God, the spirits of all flesh, of whom we have made mention, and of whom we have not made mention, who are of the true faith, from righteous Abel unto this day; do Thou Thyself give them rest there in the land of the living, in Thy kingdom, in the delight of Paradise, in the bosom of Abraham and Isaac and Jacob, our holy fathers; whence pain and grief and lamentation have fled away;

In regard to its authority Dr. Mason says:

"Probably no well-informed person doubts that prayers for the dead, and in particular prayers at the Eucharistic Sacrifice, are as ancient as Christianity itself, and have as complete a sanction as the universal custom of the Church can give. . . . . If there is but one generally acknowledged prayer for a departed Christian in the New Testament (2 Tim. i. 18), no disapproval of such prayers is either expressed or implied. The absence of them is perhaps to be explained by the expectation of Christ's immediate return, which drew away attention from the 'brief waiting of the faithful dead,' partly also by the joyful certainty of a glorious issue which the Lord's resurrection had newly shed over the waiting state."—(A. J. Mason, *Purgatory — The State of the Faithful Departed — Invocation of Saints*, pp. 59-61.)

Purgatory, as commonly taught and understood among Roman Catholics, is an unwarranted and one-sided development of a belief in an intermediate state in which the disembodied soul grows in holiness, and

---

where the light of Thy countenance looks upon them and gives them light for evermore."—F. E. Brightman, *Eastern Liturgies*, p. 57. Compare *Translations of the Primitive Liturgies*, by J. M. Neale and R. F. Littledale, where an appendix gives sixteen specimens of the more interesting among the intercessions for the departed found in early liturgies, with the two special objects (1) of proving the antiquity and catholicity of the practice, and (2) of showing the distinction between the prayers for the departed offered by the early Church, which presuppose them to be in a state of blessedness, and the later Roman doctrine of a purgatory from which the departed soul has to be delivered as from a state of misery.

so in fitness for the full joy of heaven. (See Martensen, *Christian Dogmatics*, 'The Intermediate State.')

"The departed are in God's hands; but it is possible that He may allow our prayers to help them, and we cannot point to any evil that is likely to come from such prayers, provided only that we do not allow ourselves to be led into adopting dreams and fictions concerning their condition." "God's revelation has made known to us that this other world exists; but it has not pleased God to reveal secrets in the fulness that we long for. . . . We have no right to lift the veil which He has not lifted, and it is contrary to the whole character of His revelation to put our own human imaginations by the side of the revelation itself, and to adapt our spiritual life to dreams, however beautiful. We may be sure that there is good reason why God has limited our knowledge, and we must bow to these limitations."—(Abp. Temple, *Charge*, 1898, pp. 16, 17.)

The future glory of the saints.— The future perfected glory of God's faithful servants is described in Holy Scripture under many figures. While we insist on the allegorical character of the representations, we must remember that metaphors stand for realities. Figurative descriptions are frequently employed in the Bible in order to bring home to us great spiritual truths which otherwise we could not readily grasp.

There are five chief figures round which gather the allegorical descriptions of the world to come in the Revelation of St. John, which may be regarded as an epitome of the other books of Scripture on this subject:

(1) The blessed are represented as *crowned*. The crown stands for the royalty of character which they have gained by victory over temptation. They are kings and priests unto God, ruling over things around them, as they offer themselves in perfect obedience to do His will. (Rev. ii. 10, iv. 4, i. 6; 2 Tim. iv. 8.)

(2) They are arrayed in *bright vesture*, their white robes telling of the cleanness of heart, the stainlessness of life, which at last is theirs. (Rev. iii. 5, vii. 13, 14, xix. 8.)

(3) The perpetual *music* of harp and song denotes the perfect gladness with which all service of whatever kind is rendered. (Rev. xiv. 2, 3, xxii. 3.)

(4) The unclouded *light* represents the clear and ever growing knowledge in which they rejoice as all perplexities are unravelled. (Rev. xxi. 23, xxii. 4, 5; 1 Cor. xiii. 12.)

(5) The *city* in which they are pictured as having their abode tells at once of companionship — it is no solitary life — and of the variety of employments and the opportunities for mutual service, in which they rejoice. (Rev. xxi. 2, 10-27; Eph. v. 19; Heb. xii. 22.)

"The happiness of which good men shall partake is not distinct from their godlike nature. Happiness and holiness are but two several notions of one thing."[4] That which is pictured in Holy Scripture

---

[4] Quoted from John Smith, the Cambridge Platonist, *On the Happiness and Holiness of True Religion*, by Malcolm MacColl in his *Christianity in relation to Science and Morals* (lectures on the Nicene Creed), p. 312.

ESCHATOLOGY

is "the perfect life where men, being at last perfectly what men ought to be in soul and body, live the perfect life in the perfect city; adoring God, the Three in One, with all the angelic hosts: beholding God in all things, and all things in God: enjoying all the richness of universal truth and beauty, all the joy of mutual love and fellowship and service, in a progress which can never end, where there can never be lack of novelty or variety, so infinite is the richness of the being of God in whom all spirits live."—(C. Gore, *Creed of the Christian*, p. 106.)

Eternal Life.— All this is summed up in the promise of *Life*. The life everlasting of which the Creed speaks is not equivalent merely to immortality. It stands for the true, the blessed life in the full enjoyment and exercise of all their faculties, the perfect satisfaction of all parts of their being, which shall be theirs in whom the Blessed Spirit of God has been allowed to accomplish His sanctifying work. This is the life which is life indeed, which Christ came to gain for man, which the Holy Spirit, the Life-giver, communicates, which is to be cherished and developed here, which shall have its perfect realization hereafter. (1 Tim. vi. 19; John x. 10; Rom. viii. 2, 23.)

Eternal Death.— The profession of belief in the Life Eternal, the full, true, perfect life to which the servants of God finally attain, for which God made us, Christ redeemed us, the Holy Spirit prepares us — inevitably suggests the thought of the possibility of failure. The loss of life, the absence of life where it should be found, is death. (1 John v. 16 *sq.;* Rev. iii. 14, xxi. 8.) This is the portion of those who believe not and obey not. It is not a penalty which is inflicted upon them from without, but a wreck and ruin in which they involve themselves. He that soweth to the flesh shall of the flesh reap — not annihilation but — corruption, shrivelled ears not worth the harvesting. This is what is contrasted with sowing to the spirit, and of the spirit reaping life eternal. (Gal. vi. 7, 8.)

This wreck and ruin of our nature is described in Holy Scripture, like the perfected development of our nature, under various figurative expressions. Some of these are derived from the valley of Hinnom, outside the walls of Jerusalem, which served as a charnel house, where the refuse of the city was consumed. So we are told of the unquenchable fire of God's holiness, that must torture since it was not allowed to purify the soul; and of the undying worm which represents the gnawing of remorse. (Mark ix. 43 *sq.;* Matt. v. 22.) In like manner souls are described as in outer darkness, banished from the joy of God's presence; as bound in chains of evil habit to which they allowed themselves to become enslaved; the gnashing of teeth is the image of despair. (Matt. viii. 12; 2 Pet. ii. 4; John viii. 34.)

About this doom a great deal of unwarranted teaching has been common. Many questions are apparently left unanswered in Scripture, about the number or proportion of the lost, about the nature of their suffering, and its possible mitigation. All this has been a fruitful source of not very profitable speculation.[5] Of these two points we are sure:

(1) Irretrievable and final ruin is an awful possibility. This is clear from our Lord's words. Of one He said, "Good were it for that man if he had never been born." (Matt. xxvi. 24.)[6] This saying of our Lord, if it stood alone, would seem to be decisive against the theory of Universal Restoration. If, after whatever prolonged period of purifying suffering, the soul were at length to attain final and unending beatitude, would not this make worth while any remedial discipline?

(2.) This utter and hopeless ruin can only be brought about by man's deliberate and persistent rejection of God's purpose and design. We are as sure of God's mercy as of His justice. We know that He willeth not the death of any; that He will do all He can on our behalf; but He cannot save us in spite of ourselves; He will not force our will; in doing so He would destroy man in the process of saving him. (Ezek. xxxiii. 11; John v. 39, vi. 37; 1 Tim. ii. 4.)

This life the term of probation.— So far as we are told this life is the appointed period of man's probation. On his use or misuse of his opportunities

---

[5] See an extremely thoughtful sermon, "Sin and Judgment," in Dean Church's volume, *Human Life and its Conditions*.

[6] Compare Matthew xii. 31, 32, and Newman's lines:

"Christ on Himself, considerate Master, took
The utterance of that doctrine's fearful sound,
The fount of Love His servants sends to tell
Love's deeds; Himself reveals the sinner's hell."
—(*Lyra Apostolica*, lxxxiii. "The Wrath to Come.")

here depends his future lot. A reason for this may be seen in the necessity that man's choice should be made while he is in the integrity of his complex being, with body as well as soul. The moral bent is sufficiently exhibited here. We have no warrant for teaching that it can be radically altered elsewhere.

Our final salvation depends on our union with Christ. Many leave this world without opportunity of believing on Him. We are in no way bound to suppose that these are all ultimately lost. For those who have been true to the light given them in conscience and in imperfect religious systems, God may have means in the unseen world for bringing them into union with Christ corresponding to the ministry of His Word and Sacraments, by which He communicates or offers His grace to us in this world. They are not saved by the imperfect religion which they profess; but by virtue of their obedience to the light vouchsafed, a gleam from the Light that lighteneth every man, they are prepared and fitted to accept the fuller revelation, when it is presented to them. True to the voice of the Eternal Word, though they knew not whose voice it was, they are prepared to obey Him when He is manifested to them. (John xviii. 37.)

The law of Retribution. — The final reward of the righteous and the doom of the wicked, Heaven and Hell, Life and Death, are seen to be no arbitrary appointments. They are the result of the law of Retribution, which prevails throughout the universe, material and moral, that whatsoever a man soweth that shall he also reap. We sow our thoughts and rea our actions, we sow our actions and reap our habits, we sow our habits and reap our character, we sow our character and reap our destiny. Every man will go to his own place, the place for which he has become fitted.

"Death only transplants us out of this world, with which we are so familiar, into another world: transplants us with the character which in this world we have made for ourselves unchanged, into that unfamiliar world beyond, where God is waiting to see us judge ourselves as He judges us."— (C. Gore, *The Creed of the Christian*, p. 104.)

There remains a question as to the *endlessness*, not of the loss, for that we have seen may be final and irretrievable, but of the existence of the lost, of those who have hopelessly lost their true life. Is their ruined existence necessarily indefinite, eternal? or may there be in the end a final destruction of the being which has failed of its true purpose? To this question no decided answer has been given by the Church, nor by the Scriptures on which her teaching is based. The answer must depend in part upon another question, the reply to which is perhaps more often assumed than considered: Is man by nature immortal, or is endless life (which should be distinguished from a mere survival of death) a part, while only a part, of that higher and eternal life to which man is destined to attain by his correspondence with God's grace and obedience to His law? In other words, does God necessarily uphold in endless existence a being which has forfeited its true life? Such a doctrine of conditional immortality has been held by devout men in the Christian Church. Neither Scripture nor any decree of the Church has closed the door against such an opinion. This is all that can be said.

From Thy wrath and from everlasting damnation, from the bitter pains of eternal death, good Lord deliver us, Who didst come that man might have life and have it in abundance!

BIBLIOGRAPHY

J. E. C. Welldon, " The Hope of Immortality."

S. D. F. Salmond, " The Christian Doctrine of Immortality."

C. L. Slattery, " Life beyond Life."

H. L. Goodge, " The First Epistle to the Corinthians," ch. xv. (in Westminister Commentaries.)

W. Jackson, " The Doctrine of Retribution." (Bampton Lectures, 1875.)

H. M. Luckock, " After Death."

F. W. Farrar, " Mercy and Judgment."

E. B. Pusey, "What is of Faith as to Everlasting Punishment."

E. H. Plumptre, " The Spirits in Prison."

A. J. Mason, " Purgatory — The State of the Faithful Departed — Invocation of Saints."

S. C. Gayford, " Life after death."

Edward White, " Life in Christ."

W. E. Gladstone, " Studies subsidiary to the Works of Bishop Butler," pt. II. cc. i-v.

W. R. Huntington, "Conditional Immortality."

APPENDICES

APPENDIX A

The Christian Doctrine of God

In Christianity, as nowhere else, the severed portions of truth found in all other systems are organically united, while it completes the body of truth by discoveries peculiar to itself. The Christian doctrine of God, for example, may fairly claim to be the synthesis of all the separate elements of truth found in Agnosticism, Pantheism, and Deism, which by their very antagonisms reveal themselves as one-sidednesses, requiring to be brought into some higher harmony. If Agnosticism affirms that there is that in God — in His infinite and absolute existence, which transcends finite comprehension, Christian theology does the same. If Pantheism affirms the absolute immanence of God in the world, and Deism His absolute transcendence over it, Christianity unites the two sides of the truth in a higher concept, maintaining at the same time the Divine immanence and the Divine transcendence.

Even Polytheism in its nobler forms is in its own dark way a witness for a truth which a hard, abstract Monotheism, such as we have in the later (not the Biblical) Judaism, and in Mohammedanism, ignores — the truth, namely, that God is plurality as well as unity — that in Him there is a manifoldness of life, a fulness and diversity of powers and manifestations, such as is expressed by the word Elohim. This element of truth in Polytheism Christianity also takes up, and sets in its proper relation to the unity of God in its doctrine of Tri-unity — the concept of God which is distinctively the Christian one, and which furnishes the surest safeguard of a living Theism against the extremes of both Pantheism and Deism. . . .

To take a last example, Positivism is a very direct negation of Christianity; yet in its strange 'worship of Humanity' is there not that which stretches across the gulf and touches hands with a religion which meets the cravings of the heart for the *human* in God by the doctrine of the Incarnation?

It is the part of a true and wise theology to take account of all this, and to seek, with ever-increasing enlargement of vision, the comprehensive view in which all factors of the truth are combined.—(James Orr, *The Christian view of God and the World*, pp. 12, 13.)

APPENDIX B

EVOLUTION AND CREATION

Since the hypothesis of Evolution is nothing else than an attempt to explain *how* the heavens and the earth were created, leaving the statement quite untouched that they *were* created, it is difficult to see how the two notions can come into collision with one another. The one simply takes up the story where the other leaves it off. And we have only to place them end to end, thus: 'From God all things took their origin; and by successive stages of evolution He made them to become what they now are:' in order to see quite clearly how the ancient and the modern statements are merely one line prolonged. We may, therefore, decline to argue (as is frequently done) that the Evolution theory remains at present in a very precarious condition — though the allegation is true. For I hold it quite unworthy of Christians to show any slight, or even to accord a reluctant acceptance, to the only theory of Creation which has hitherto thrown any light on this mysterious subject. For it is not light, it is darkness, to say (with the ancient sages) 'water is the first principle of all things,' or 'fire is the first principle,' or 'all things come out of a cosmic egg,' or 'the world came forth by an oversight while Brahma slept.' Nor is it sufficient to assert, with the ancient Hebrews, that 'Jehovah spake the word and all things were made.' The question now raised by Science is the further question, 'What, more precisely, did Jehovah speak? What were the laws which proceeded out of His mouth?' And if it should be ascertained — as it promises to be — that the creative laws, which have produced all this marvellous complexity we find around us, were the same on a vast scale as those which we see with our eyes at work on a small scale; if it should appear that births, not startling apparitions, have throughout been God's method; that His laws have always been laws of growth (as we know it in the crystal, the plant, the animal), not of abrupt finality; and that steadfast continuity of plan has characterized creation, not a fitful and feeble caprice; surely all these discoveries come home to us as, in the highest sense, human, rational, intelligible. The conception of the primal creative 'word' is now expanded into that of a majestic stream of legislation, permeating and controlling all things; the creative 'fiat' is rescued from humiliating comparison with a magician's potent spell; and the statement becomes for the first time clear and comprehensible, that 'by the WORD — the Logos, or intelligible reason — of God, all things in heaven and earth were made.'— (G. H. Curteis, *The Scientific Obstacles to Christian Belief*, pp. 56-58, Boyle Lectures, 1884.)

APPENDIX C

Possession by Evil Spirits

It is argued that in the matter of possession by evil spirits Christ was only using the ordinary phraseology of His time; that diseases which we now place under the head of hysteria, hypochondria, lunacy, etc., were then ascribed to the direct agency of evil spirits; and that, according to His usual plan, Christ made no attempt to change the popular conviction. Of course there is no theoretical objection to applying this principle in this case, provided it be certain that there is no such difference in it compared with the others [such as the critical questions connected with the authorship of the books of the Old Testament] as will render the application of the rule misleading. But it is by no means clear that this is so. The existence of the Evil One and of spirits of evil is not altogether a matter for the scientific understanding to verify. It is in large measure a moral question.

I. Every man is conscious in a more or less degree of temptations — that is, of positive incitements to evil. These may be explained in two ways — either as the suggestions of our own lower nature, or as provocations from without. In the first case, we ourselves are the whole and sole cause of the suggestion; for the motions of the lower nature are just as much ours as those of the higher. We cannot, as

Aristotle observed, make ourselves responsible for our good actions only. It is plain that if this be so, temptation cannot occur to us without a certain degree of sinful acquiescence; we are tempted when we give ear to the suggestions of the lower part of ourselves. On the other hand, there is in moral natures of a powerful kind a firm conviction of violent struggle, not only with the lower part of self, but with a mighty and masterful will. It is doubtless true that a consciousness akin to this occurs in persons of a nervous and hysterical temperament; but it stands in their case to the conviction of a saint, as sentimentality stands to constant love. And we believe that the conviction of a struggle with a masterful will increases rather than diminishes in proportion to the strength and acuteness of the character, so that in a mind enlightened by perpetual communion with the Father, and incapable of producing suggestions of evil from within, it reaches a point at which no doubt could be possible.

II. In nature also, there are certainly signs of a wrong influence at work; not merely of a feeble realization of the laws of being, but of positive ruin and evil. To attribute all this to the action of God would be profane, to the action of man would be impossible. A third possibility remains, therefore, one which has the authority of Scripture upon its side, as well as a large body of human belief, that an evil spirit is at work in the world as well as in the secret chambers of the heart, to whom some at any rate of the evil in nature is due. The whole subject is profoundly mysterious and obscure, the one thing which is clear about it being this, that the existence of the Evil One, and of those spirits who follow his lead, is a question which none of our senses can settle; it must depend upon the exercise of those powers in us which enable us to distinguish physical and moral evil.

If these contentions be held valid, it would follow that our Lord in ascribing certain physical ailments to the direct agency of evil spirits, and not others, and in revealing the history of His own Temptation, must not be regarded merely as adopting current phraseology, but as really exercising His own moral insight. The difference between this point of view and that of science might possibly be settled by an extension of our scientific knowledge; some of the cases now assigned to merely physical causes may, hereafter, be allowed to be manifestations of the powers of darkness.—(T. B. Strong, *A Manual of Theology*, pp. 126-128.)

APPENDIX D

The Incarnation

The self-same Person, or Ego, who had dwelt in the bosom of the Father as Son or Word, and as God from, in, and with the Father, did in the Incarnation attach manhood to His Godhead — did, without compromising His divine life, enter into the conditions of human life, and surround Himself, so to speak, with a new sphere of being and action: so that the work of redemption was wrought, not by a holy human individual in close alliance with the Eternal Son and thoroughly penetrated by the Spirit, but by the very Eternal Son Himself, clothed in humanity, but retaining His personality inviolate, and therewith the attributes or perfections which in truth 'are Himself,' although for the most part making them ineffective, or suspending their activity, within the limits involved in the assumption of 'the form of a servant.' Thus, according to this grand belief, did the one Christ bring God and man together by virtue of which His preëxisting divinity and of the humanity which for our sakes He put on.—(W. Bright, *The Age of the Fathers*, Vol. II. p. 258.)

"The Word was made flesh." (John i. 14.)

The following main truths must be held as expressed in the words when they are fairly interpreted:

(1) The Lord's humanity was complete, as against various forms of Apollinarianism, according to which the divine Logos supplied the place of part of that which belongs to the perfection of Manhood [*i. e.* a rational soul]. (The Word became *flesh*, and not *a body* or the like.)

(2) The Lord's humanity was real and permanent, as against various forms of Gnosticism, according to which He only assumed in appearance, or for a time, that which was and remained foreign to Himself. (The Word *became* flesh, and did not *clothe Himself in* flesh.)

(3) The Lord's human and divine natures remained without change, each fulfilling its part according to its proper laws, as against various forms of Eutychianism, according to which the result of the Incarnation is a third nature, if the humanity has any real existence. (The *Word* became *flesh*, both terms being preserved side by side.)

(4) The Lord's humanity was universal and not individual, as including all that belongs to the essence of man, without regard to sex or race or time. (The Word became *flesh* and not *a man.*)

(5) The Lord's human and divine natures were united in one Person, as against various forms of Nestorianism, according to which He has a human personality and a divine personality, to which the acts, etc., belonging to the respective natures must be referred. (*The Word became flesh and dwelt, etc.*, without any change of the subject to the verb.)

(6) The Word did not acquire personality by the Incarnation. He is spoken of throughout, not as a principle or an energy, but, whatever may be the inherent imperfection of such language, as a Person.

So far, perhaps, we can see generally a little of the Truth, but the attempt to express the Truth with precision is beset with difficulty and even with peril. Thus in using the words 'personality' and 'impersonal' in relation to Christ, it is obviously necessary to maintain the greatest reserve. For us 'personality' implies limitation or determination, *i. e.* finiteness in some direction. As applied to the divine nature therefore the word is not more than a necessary accommodation required to give such distinctness to our ideas as may be attainable. The word 'impersonal,' again, as applied to the Lord's human nature, is not to be so understood as to exclude in any way the right application of the word 'man' ($\mathring{\alpha}\nu\theta\rho\omega\pi\sigma$) to Him, as it is used both by Himself (John viii. 40) and by St. Paul (1 Tim. ii. 5).

The phrase *The Word became flesh* is absolutely unique. The phrases which point towards it in St. John (1 John iv. 2), in the Epistle to the Hebrews (ii. 14), and in St. Paul (Rom. viii. 3, Phil. ii. 7, 1 Tim. iii. 16) fall short of the majestic fulness of this brief sentence, which affirms once for all the reconciliation of the opposite elements of the final antithesis of life and thought, the finite and the infinite.— (B. F. Westcott, *The Gospel according to St. John*, p. 11.)

APPENDIX E

SCRIPTURE AND CHURCH AUTHORITY

For religious and simple minds there is a short method whereby to put off error, and to discover and extract the truth. For if we return to the head and original of Divine tradition, human error ceases; and having seen into the grounds of the heavenly sacraments, whatever lay hid under the gloom and cloud of darkness, is laid open to the light of truth. If a conduit conveying water, which before flowed copiously and abundantly, should suddenly fail, do we not go to the fountain, that there the reason of the failure may be ascertained, whether the springs having failed, the water has dried up at the fountain-head; or whether, flowing thence in unimpaired fulness, it is stopped in the middle of its course; that so, if through the defect of leaks or obstructions in the conduit the water supplied have been hindered from flowing in a continuous and unbroken stream, then, the conduit being repaired and strengthened, the water, kept together, may be supplied for the use and consumption of the city in the same abundance and fulness wherewith it issues from the fountain? This then it now behoves the priests of God to do who keep the Divine commandments, that if the truth has in any respect tottered and faltered, we should go back to our Lord, as our head, and to the Evangelic and

Apostolic tradition; that so the grounds of our action might spring thence, whence both our order and origin took its rise.— (St. Cyprian (A. D. 256), Epistle lxxiv, to Pompeius.)

I submit myself and my poor endeavours, first, to the judgment of the Catholic œcumenical essential Church; which if some of late dates have endeavoured to hiss out of the schools as a fancy, I cannot help it. From the beginning it was not so. And if I should mistake the right Catholic Church out of human frailty or ignorance (which for my part I have no reason in the world to suspect; yet it is not impossible, when the Romanists themselves are divided into five or six several opinions, what this Catholic Church, or what their infallible judge is), I do implicitly and in the preparation of my mind submit myself to the true Catholic Church, the spouse of Christ, the mother of saints, 'the pillar of Truth.' And seeing my adherence is firmer to the infallible rule of Faith, that is, the Holy Scriptures interpreted by the Catholic Church, than to mine own private judgment or opinions; although I should unwillingly fall into an error; yet this cordial submission is an implicit retractation thereof, and I am confident will be so accepted by the Father of Mercies, both from me and all others who seriously and sincerely do seek after peace and truth.

Likewise I submit myself to the representative Church, that is, a free general Council, or so general as can be procured; and until then, to the Church of England, wherein I was baptized, or to a national

English Synod: to the determination of all which, and each of them respectively, according to the distinct degrees of their authority, I yield a conformity and compliance, or at the least, and to the lowest of them, an acquiescence.—(Abp. Bramhall (A. D. 1656), preface to the *Reply to the R. C. Bishop of Chalcedon*, Works, Vol. II, p. 22.)

APPENDIX F

PREDESTINATION AND ELECTION

There are two ideas commonly associated with predestination which St. Paul gives us no warrant for asserting. The one is the predestination of individuals to eternal loss or destruction. That God should create any single individual with the intention of eternally destroying or punishing him is a horrible idea, and, without prying into mysteries, we may say boldly, that there is no warrant for it in the Old or New Testaments. God is indeed represented as predestinating men, like Jacob and Esau, to a higher or lower place in the order of the world or the church. There are 'vessels' made by the divine potter to purposes of 'honour,' and 'vessels' made to purposes (comparatively) of 'dishonour:' there are more honourable and less honourable limbs of the body. (Rom. ix. 21; 1 Cor. xii. 22, etc.) But this does not prejudice the eternal prospects of those who in this world hold the less advantageous posts. With God is no respect of persons.

Again God is represented as predestinating men to moral hardness of heart where such hardness is a judgment on previous wilfulness. Thus men may be predestined to temporary rejection of God, as in St. Paul's mind the majority of the contemporary Jews were. That was their judgment, and their punishment. (Comp. St. Matt. xiii. 13-15; St. John xii.

39, 40.) It was however not God's first intention for them nor His last. . . . (Rom. xi. 29, 32; 1 Tim. ii. 4.)

Once again, the idea of a predestination for good, taking effect necessarily and irrespective of men's coöperation, is an idea which has been intruded unjustifiably into St. Paul's thought. It exalts his whole being tò consider that he is coöperating with God, and that the conditions under which he lives represent a divine purpose with which he is called to work. . . . but he never suggests that it does not lie within the mysterious power of his own will to withdraw himself from coöperation with God. It is at least conceivable to him that he should himself be rejected (1 Cor. ix. 27). . . .

Certainly when St. Paul dwells upon the thought of divine predestination he dwells upon it in order to emphasize that through all the vicissitudes of the world's history, a divine purpose runs; and especially that God works out His universal purposes through specially selected agents, 'His elect,' on whom His choice rests for special ends in accordance with an eternal design and intention. And the sense of coöperating with an eternal purpose of God inspires and strengthens him. For God will not drop His work by the way. . . . (Rom. viii. 28-30; Phil. i. 6.)

This predestinated body, the Church, is what in another word St. Paul calls the 'elect' or 'chosen.' The idea of election has had a very false turn given to it, partly through mistakes which have been already alluded to, partly because the idea of election has been separated from another idea with which in the Bible it is most clearly associated, the idea of a universal purpose to which the elect minister. No thought can be more prominent in the Old Testament than the thought that some men out of multitudes have been chosen by God to be in a special relation of intimacy with Him. 'You only have I known, O Israel, of all the families of the earth.' But this election to special knowledge of God, and special spiritual opportunity, carries with it a corresponding responsibility. . . . 'You only have I known of all the families of the earth; therefore will I visit upon you all your iniquities.' (Amos iii. 2.) The fact is that the principle of inequality in capacity and opportunity runs through the whole world both in individuals and in societies. A great genius or a great nation, has special privileges and opportunities, but also in the sight of God, who judges men according to their opportunities, special responsibilities. But also (and this is by far the most important point) the special vocation of every elect individual or body is for the sake of others. It is God's method to work through the few upon the many. That is the law of ministry which binds all the world of strong and weak, of rich and poor, of learned and ignorant, into one. Thus Abraham had been chosen alone, but it was that, through his seed, all the nations of the earth should be blessed. Israel was exclusively the people of God, but it was in order that all nations should learn from them at last the word of God. The apostles were the first 'elect' in Christ with a little Jewish company. 'We'— so St. Paul speaks of the Jewish Christians —'we who had before hoped in

Christ.' But it was to show the way to all the Gentiles ('ye also, who have heard the word of the truth, the gospel of your salvation'), who were also to constitute 'God's own possession' and His 'heritage.' The purpose to be realized is a universal one: it is the reunion of man with man, as such, by being all together reunited to God in one body.—(Chas. Gore, *The Epistle to the Ephesians*, pp. 64-71.)

APPENDIX G

PHYSICAL DEATH AND ITS CONNECTION WITH SIN

It may be urged by a biologist, 'The fact of physical death is inextricably interwoven into the structural growth of the world long before men appeared. But Christianity regards it as a mere consequence of human sin.' This is not the case. Long before science had investigated the early history of life on our globe, Christian teachers both in East and in West — St. Augustine as well as St. Athanasius — had taught that death is the law of physical nature, that it had been in the world before man, and 'man was by nature mortal,' because, as being animal, he was subject to death. How then do they interpret the language of Scripture? In this way: They hold that if man had been true to his spiritual nature, the supernatural life, the life in God, would have blunted the forces of corruption, and lifted him into a higher and immortal state.

Certainly, in some sense, death, as we know it, for man, is regarded, especially in the New Testament, as the penalty of sin. But then what do we mean by death? If sin is said to have introduced human death, Christ is constantly said to have abolished it. 'This is the bread that cometh down from heaven, that a man may eat thereof and not die.' 'Whosoever believeth on me shall never die.' 'Christ Jesus abolished death.' Sin, then, we may suppose, only introduced death in some sense such as that in which Christ abolished it. Christ has not abolished the physical transition from this world to the invisible world, but He has robbed it of its terror, its sting, its misery. Apart from sin we may suppose man would not have died; that is, he would never have had that horrible experience which he has called death. There would have been only some transition full of a glorious hope from one state of being to another.

We are in the region of conjecture. All that I am here interested in asserting is that Christianity never has held to the position that human sin first introduced death *into the world*. What it has taught is that *human* death, as men have known it, with its horror and its misery, has represented not God's intention for man, but the curse of sin. — (Chas. Gore, *The Epistle to the Romans*, Vol. II. Note E.)

APPENDIX H

Eternal Life and Its Loss

The leading office of the Gospel, in its bearing on the world to come, was to make known, not misery, but salvation. Its direct concern was with the moral and spiritual part of man; the part in which he had received a deadly wound; the part which supplies the true enduring basis of what he *is*, the basis of his character. To heal that wound, to supply that character with a fund of enduring vitality, it did not furnish him with particular information as to the conditions of the life to come: but, leaving his ignorance to be dispelled at the proper season when it shall arrive, revealed the one great secret which comprised in itself every other that concerned him, the mode and means of his reunion with God.

But in the shadow of this glorious teaching lay another inevitable question: What shall be the lot of those who reject it? This question was small and remote for the hundred and twenty elect souls in the upper room, set upon pursuance of the truth and the right. But it gradually grew large and larger still for the Church, as it spread from land to land, and obtained the world's confessed, or professed allegiance. The provision for meeting this question was ready to hand. It lay, in a certain sense, outside the Gospel; and was anterior to it, like other laws of our human nature, and of the government of the world by its Author. But this law, like all other antecedent and perpetual laws, was acknowledged by the Gospel; it was the law of 'indignation and wrath, tribulation and anguish, upon every soul of man that doeth evil.' (Rom. ii. 8, 9.) But it was acknowledged with a sorrow which is shown by the comparatively fluctuating or shadowy manner in which this sad reverse of the picture is presented; the inseparable but obscure underside, so to speak, of the great foundation-stone of our peace and happiness. How much do we know of the lot of the perversely wicked? They disappear into pain and sorrow; the veil drops upon them in that condition. Every indication of a further change is withheld; so that, if it be designed, it has not been made known, and is nowhere incorporated with the Divine teaching. Whatever else pertains to this sad subject is withheld from our too curious and unprofitable gaze. If men cannot restrain their thoughts, their affections, from further speculation, let them take good heed that, as it is necessarily weak and shadowy, so it be deeply tinged with modesty and awe.

Let there not be the presumption of assimilating hope or surmise with the solid truth of the great revelation. The specific and limited statements supplied to us are, after all, only expressions in particular form of immovable and universal laws, on the one hand, of the irrevocable union between suffering and sin; on the other, of the perfection of the Most High; both of them believed in full, but only in part disclosed and having elsewhere, it may be, their plenary manifestation, in that day of the restitution of all things, for which a groaning and travailing creation yearns.—(W. E. Gladstone, *Studies subsidiary to the works of Bishop Butler*, pt. II. ch. iv.)

www.ingramcontent.com/pod-product-compliance
Lightning Source LLC
Chambersburg PA
CBHW072138160426
43197CB00012B/2159